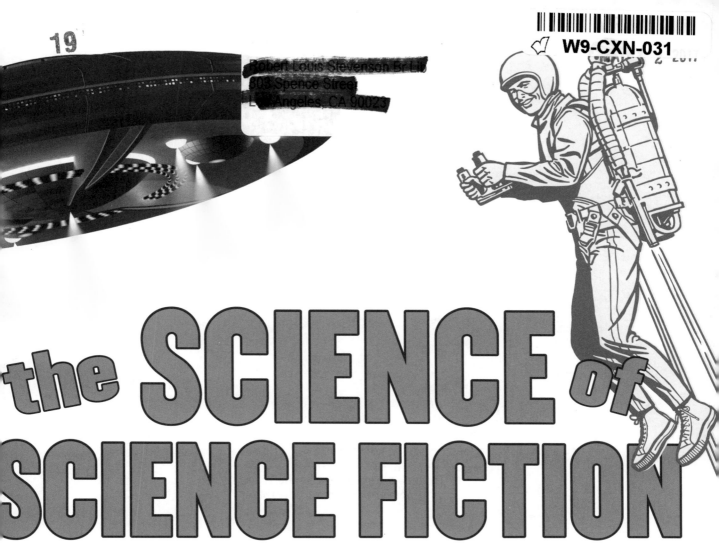

19

W9-CXN-031

the SCIENCE of SCIENCE FICTION

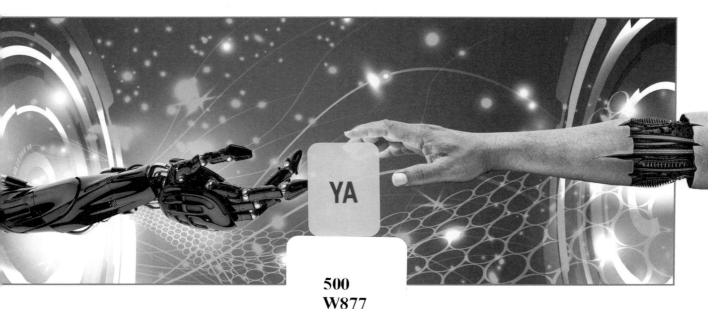

YA

INQUIRE AND INVESTIGATE

Matthew Brenden Wood
Illustrated by Tom Casteel

Nomad Press
A division of Nomad Communications
10 9 8 7 6 5 4 3 2 1

This book was manufactured by CGB Printers,
North Mankato, Minnesota, United States
February 2017, Job #216317
ISBN Softcover: 978-1-61930-470-3
ISBN Hardcover: 978-1-61930-466-6

Educational Consultant, Marla Conn

Questions regarding the ordering of this book should be addressed to
Nomad Press
2456 Christian St.
White River Junction, VT 05001
www.nomadpress.net

More science titles in the
Inquire and Investigate series

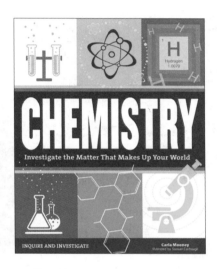

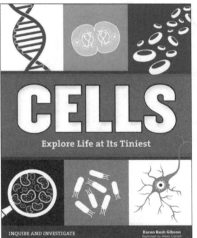

Check out more titles at www.nomadpress.net

Interested in primary sources?

PS

Look for this icon.

You can use a smartphone or tablet app to scan the QR codes and explore more about science fiction! Cover up neighboring QR codes to make sure you're scanning the right one. You can find a list of URLs on the Resources page.

If the QR code doesn't work, try searching the Internet with the Keyword Prompts to find other helpful sources. 🔍 science fiction

Contents ▶

TIMELINE

Sci-Fi - 1903   Massive "land ironclads," or tanks, appear in "The Land Ironclads" by H.G. Wells
1917 .... First tank battle, World War I

Sci-Fi - 1911   Television, radar, and solar energy appear in *Ralph 124c 41+* by Hugo Gernsback
1939 .... First radar system deployed in England

Sci-Fi - 1914   The atomic bomb is introduced in *The World Set Free* by H.G. Wells
1945 .... First atomic bomb detonated in New Mexico desert

Sci-Fi - 1888   People purchase items without cash in *Looking Backward: 2000–1887* by Edward Bellamy
1950 .... First Diner's Club Cards issued

Sci-Fi - 1870   Captain Nemo pilots an electric submarine in *20,000 Leagues Under the Sea* by Jules Verne
1954 .... *USS Nautilus*, the first nuclear submarine, launched

Sci-Fi - 1865   Three explorers journey to the moon in a capsule launched from Earth in *From the Earth to the Moon by* Jules Verne
1969 .... First astronauts walk on the moon

Sci-Fi - 1966   Personal "communicators" appear on the TV show *Star Trek*
1973 .... First cell phone call

Sci-Fi - 1948   Microwaveable meals are cooked in *Space Cadet* by Robert Heinlein
1986 .... First microwaveable frozen dinners

Sci-Fi - 1989   Virtual reality headsets are used for entertainment in the movie *Back to the Future Part II*
1995 .... Nintendo Virtual Boy is first home VR set

Sci-Fi - 1990   A worldwide network of information connects everyone and everything in *Earth* by David Brin
1995 .... Netscape and Internet Explorer become popular web browsers

Sci-Fi - 1932   Genetic engineering and cloning appear in *Brave New World* by Aldous Huxley
1996 .... Dolly the sheep is the first animal to be cloned from an adult cell

TIMELINE

Sci-Fi - 1951 A robot beats a human at chess in *Time and Again* by Clifford Simak
1997 .... Deep Blue, a computer, beats human chess grandmaster Garry Kasparov

Sci-Fi - 1953 In-ear radios deliver music and news in *Fahrenheit 451* by Ray Bradbury
2001 .... Earbuds become popular headphones

Sci-Fi - 1968 Video calls, space tourism, and tablet computers are showcased in the movie *2001: A Space Odyssey*
2003 .... Apps such as Skype are introduced

Sci-Fi - 1961 Electronic, touchscreen books appear in *Return from the Stars* by Stanislaw Lem
2007 .... First popular eReaders become available

Sci-Fi - 1977 Ion engine–powered spacecraft appears in the movie *Star Wars: A New Hope*
2007 .... Ion engine powers *DAWN* spacecraft to asteroids Vespa, Ceres

Sci-Fi - 2002 Gestures are used to interact with technology in the movie *Minority Report*
2010 .... Microsoft Kinect released for Xbox

Sci-Fi - 1946 Detective Dick Tracy uses a two-way wrist radio in the comic book *Dick Tracy*
2014 .... Smartwatches become common

Sci-Fi - 1987 Replicators can construct almost anything in the movie *Star Trek: The Next Generation*
2014 .... Astronauts on the International Space Station use a 3D printer to print a wrench

Sci-Fi - 1990 Dinosaurs are brought back to life in *Jurassic Park* by Michael Crichton
2014 .... Revive and Restore founded to bring back extinct species

Sci-Fi - 1958 Completely immersive, life-like videogames are played in *The City and the Stars* by Arthur C. Clarke
2015 .... Virtual reality headsets become available

Sci-Fi - 1979 Babel fish placed in the ear translates any language in *The Hitchhiker's Guide to the Galaxy* by Douglas Adams
2015 .... Real-time translation apps are widely available

Introduction ▶

The Science Behind Science Fiction

How are science and
science fiction related?

Fantastical science fiction inspires real-life science, and it works the other way, too. Inspired by the moon landing, writers and filmmakers imagine entire new worlds with distant planets, space travel, and aliens.

Have you ever read a science fiction book or seen a science fiction movie? Science fiction is a very popular genre that imagines what life might be like for characters if certain scientific premises were real, such as artificial intelligence, humans living on Mars, and time travel. Sometimes, it can seem as though the plots portrayed in science fiction actually end up coming true in real life.

In the late 1860s, a group called the Baltimore Gun Club built a gigantic gun they named the Columbiad and pointed it straight up. With the huge rifle ready to fire, three daring adventurers climbed aboard their bullet-shaped craft and shot themselves into space. Their target was the moon.

Unfortunately, neither the Baltimore Gun Club nor their incredible cannon were real. They were the inventions of French author Jules Verne, whose 1865 novel *From the Earth to the Moon* is considered to be one of the first science fiction stories.

Although the book was fiction, many details in it were based on scientific fact. Verne positioned the great gun in Florida, reasoning that when aiming for the moon, a southerly location would be best to take advantage of the earth's rotation. He imagined the spacecraft would have sophisticated environmental control systems to give his travelers fresh air and a cozy temperature.

He even described small rockets on the outside of the capsule that would adjust its course in flight.

On their imaginary journey, Verne's three passengers encountered weightlessness, solved technical problems, and experienced the frigid shadow cast by the moon as they circled past the lunar far side. In the sequel to his novel, Verne had his explorers fire their rockets to slow their speed before splashing down in the Pacific Ocean. The fictional trio was given a hero's welcome and celebrated around the world for their incredible and daring feat. Does this sound like something that could happen in real life?

In the 1920s, a German engineer named Wernher von Braun read *From the Earth to the Moon* and was inspired to build a rocket large enough to make Verne's fictional adventure into a real one. He helped design and develop a rocket called the V-2 for the Germans during World War II.

After the war, von Braun was brought to the United States as part of Operation Paperclip. This was an effort by the U.S. government to bring more than 1,500 scientists and engineers to this country after the war. Many years later, in 1969, his 363-foot-tall rocket, named *Saturn V*, launched three men toward the moon from NASA's Cape Canaveral launch site in Florida.

SCI-FI FACT

The term "science fiction" dates back to 1851, when it was used to describe a story, novel, or poem with a scientific plot.

TO THE MOON!

Every successful invention comes after many unsuccessful attempts. Wernher von Braun was no stranger to failure. You can see footage of both his successes and failed attempts here. You can also catch a glimpse of him—he's the tall man who is not dressed in a military uniform.

What do you do when you encounter failure? What do you learn from it?

German V-2 rocket test failures

Two of the crew, Neil Armstrong and Buzz Aldrin, landed on the moon and walked on its surface before all three returned home in a spacecraft called *Columbia*. After they splashed down safely in the Pacific Ocean, the astronauts were given a hero's welcome and were known worldwide as the first men to walk on the moon.

> The amazing similarities between Verne's fiction and von Braun's fact are part of what makes science fiction so exciting.

Even though *From the Earth to the Moon* was written more than 150 years ago, it has many of the same characteristics of modern science fiction books and movies. Adventure, discovery, and danger are paired with new technology to make the impossible seem possible. And real life is still taking some of its cues from this new science fiction.

For example, a telecommunications company called Qualcomm is offering $10 million to the inventor of a real-life tricorder. This is a small, portable medical device used on the sci-fi television show *Star Trek* to quickly diagnose problems and monitor vital health information.

In other news, biologists inspired by the *Jurassic Park* franchise are working on the real science needed to create a woolly mammoth. This hairy cousin of the elephant last walked the earth 4,000 years ago.

In *The Science of Science Fiction*, you'll examine six exciting themes: resurrecting extinct species, artificial intelligence, living on other worlds, faster-than-light travel, traveling through time, and searching for aliens. Each chapter explores the fiction, fact, and future of these ideas. You'll also discover how you can take part in real-life science by joining a citizen science project hunting for planets beyond our solar system, extracting your DNA in your own kitchen, and calculating the speed of light using chocolate, a ruler, and a microwave.

From stories of resurrected dinosaurs terrorizing park-goers to a tale about a lonely astronaut trying to survive on Mars, there is always an element of truth in science fiction. In this book, you will examine the facts behind the fiction. You'll discover where science is today, and where it might be headed tomorrow. Sometimes, the worlds of our dreams are closer than we think.

KEY QUESTIONS

- Science fiction is extremely popular. Why do you think people like to read and watch science fiction?

- Have you ever been inspired by books, articles, movies, or other media that you've read or watched? What inspired you?

VOCAB LAB

There is a lot of new vocabulary in this book! Turn to the glossary in the back when you come to a word you don't understand. Practice your new vocabulary in the **Vocab Lab** activities in each chapter.

VOCAB LAB

Write down what you think each of the following words means. What root words can you find for help?

weightlessness, **feat**, **Operation Paperclip**, **artificial intelligence**, **fiction**, and **resurrect**.

Compare your definitions with those of your friends or classmates. Did you all come up with the same meanings? Turn to the text and glossary if you need help.

Chapter 1 ▶
Cloning Ancient Creatures

Is it possible to clone dinosaurs and other long-extinct creatures?

While dinosaurs are likely to stay extinct, there is a chance that scientists can clone other creatures if they can find viable DNA.

In science fiction, dinosaurs aren't always extinct. They roam around island amusement parks and generally terrorize the humans that get in their way. Most often, dinosaurs return to life in fictional universes such as that of the *Jurassic Park* franchise through cloning. This is a process through which geneticists can make clones, or copies, of long-dead organisms.

There is real science behind de-extinction, which is the term used to describe bringing extinct species back to life. Scientists have been successfully cloning both plants and animals for many years.

So why can't we visit a Tyrannosaurus rex at the zoo or take a tiny Composognathus out for a walk? While making clones is a real scientific process, cloning long-extinct species is much harder than science fiction makes it seem.

WHAT IS A GENE, ANYWAY?

Before we can talk about clones, we have to talk about what makes us unique. Much of our characteristics are determined by genes. In humans, they help determine traits such as eye and hair color. Genes are like a microscopic blueprint for every living plant or animal, from a blue whale to a dandelion. And if you have a blueprint, you just might be able to build something.

Genes are composed of DNA, which is made of millions of molecules stored inside cells. DNA contains four basic building blocks called bases, and they are named adenine, guanine, cytosine, and thymine. These bases join together in pairs—adenine with thymine and guanine with cytosine. Each pair forms between two strands and looks similar to the rungs of a ladder. That DNA ladder is twisted into a shape called a double helix.

The tightly coiled strands of DNA inside a cell contain so much information that, despite their microscopic size, they would still stretch to more than 6 feet in length! All organisms have DNA, from bacteria to bison to blueberries. This gives every organism a unique set of instructions that determines what it becomes. If you were able to make a copy of an organism's DNA, you'd be able to build a new one with the exact characteristics as the original—a clone.

CLONING THE REAL WORLD

Cloning is the process of copying the DNA of one creature and using it to create a new, genetically identical being. In *Star Wars,* clones of Jango Fett are used to create the deadly clone trooper army. Here on Earth, we can find clones in a much less sinister place—the supermarket.

Even if we were able to bring a Tyrannosaurus Rex back to life, should we?

CLONE THYSELF

A newly discovered lizard in Vietnam reproduces without a mate. Leiolepis ngovantrii, like nearly 1 percent of all lizards, can spontaneously create offspring though parthenogenesis, which is reproduction without fertilization. The resulting lizards are all females and are clones of the original female parent. Parthenogenesis happens in many kinds of species, from aphids to sharks.

Have you ever wondered why most bananas look the same? That's because genetically, they are! The typical banana you can get at a grocery store is a variety called the Cavendish, and it's a clone. The original Cavendish banana was chosen for its taste, hardiness, and resistance to disease. It is grown all over the world. These traits made the Cavendish very attractive to banana growers, and as a result it has become the most popular banana.

Making a clone of a banana isn't hard to do. Growers take suckers, or offshoots, from adult plants and supply them with the nutrients they need to grow. Those suckers become adult plants that are genetically identical to the original plant.

[
The next time you have a banana split, you can call it a clone split!
]

Clones are everywhere in nature. Some species even have the ability to clone themselves if the conditions are right. However, cloning animals is a lot more difficult and complicated than cloning plants. Animals don't have suckers or offshoots that can be trimmed and planted. But with a little help from science, it can still be done.

THE MOST FAMOUS CLONE

On July 5, 1996, Dolly the sheep was born at the Roslin Institute in Edinburgh, Scotland. Normally, the birth of a sheep is no cause for celebration in Scotland, but Dolly was different—she was the first animal clone created from an adult. This was the first time a copy of a fully grown and living animal had ever been made.

THE CAVENDISH IN DANGER

There's one major drawback to cloning bananas. Because the banana supply has no genetic diversity, all Cavendish bananas are susceptible to the same disease. A fungus called Tropical Race 4, which infects and kills banana plants, can be carried on a tiny amount of soil that could fit on the bottom of a farmer's shoe. So far, scientists have found no way of stopping its spread. This is what happened to the Cavendish's predecessor, the Gros Michel. It was wiped out by a strain of Tropical Race 4 in the 1960s. You can read more about this fungus here.

NPR doomed banana

Dolly was the clone of a six-year-old Finn Dorset sheep, and was the only lamb born out of more than 250 attempts. To create Dolly, scientists injected udder nuclei from the original sheep into the unfertilized egg cells of a second sheep. This is a process called nuclear transfer. These egg cells had their nuclei removed, and when they were exposed to electric pulses, the udder and egg cells joined. Once merged, the cells began to divide.

When scientists were sure that the cells were dividing properly, the egg cells were placed in a third, surrogate sheep, one with different coloring from the original donor sheep. That way scientists could tell just by looking that the surrogate sheep's DNA didn't end up in the cloned sheep's genetic makeup. After a normal 148-day gestation period, Dolly was born.

Since Dolly, many other animals have been cloned from adult cells, including cats, pigs, and horses. Cloning isn't done just to bring back the family cat or recreate the fastest race horse. Geneticists use clones to help understand how genes determine traits, as well as help discover more about genetic diseases so that scientists can develop treatments.

If scientists can clone animals from pretty much any adult cell, where are all the dinosaur clones? To create a clone, cells with intact DNA are needed. Obtaining DNA from living organisms is easy—there are billions of cells to choose from. But dinosaurs have been extinct for millions of years. How do we get viable, or intact, DNA from creatures that took their last breath long before humans even existed?

SCI-FI FACT

You can even pay to have your favorite pet cloned! The first cloned pet was a cat that was produced in 2004. The owner paid $50,000 for this service.

CLONING AND CONTROVERSY

When Dolly was born, it caused a stir across the world. Some people feared that cloned animals meant that the cloning of human beings was right around the corner. Others believed the knowledge that cloning provided would save lives. This sparked a debate about the ethics of cloning. Watch a news report of the event here.

🔍 Retroreport Dolly

WHAT HAPPENED TO THE DINOSAURS?

About 65 million years ago, something big happened on Earth. A huge meteorite struck our planet, sending dust and debris high into the atmosphere. This dust blocked the sun and caused temperatures around the globe to drop. Climate change at this scale caused a massive extinction of plant species. Without a food source, herbivores began to die off as well. The carnivores that ate the herbivores soon followed.

Scientists estimate that in the wake of the impact, between 50 and 90 percent of all species on Earth went extinct within about 30,000 years. Dinosaurs, the largest and most dominant animals at the time, all but disappeared from the planet. Now, all we have left of dinosaurs are their fossils.

One of the most important tools for paleontologists are fossils. When plants and animals die, the natural process of decay sets in. Soft tissues, such as organs and skin, quickly rot, while harder, denser materials, such as teeth and bone, remain behind. Those harder remains can slowly disappear as well, unless something rare happens.

Animals whose remains are buried beneath sediment in lakes, rivers, oceans, and streams decay much more slowly. During the course of many years, the sediment can harden into stone, encasing the remaining bones and teeth. As more and more sediment piles on the stone that holds the skeleton, the pressure increases. Water is forced into the spaces with the bones, which are slowly dissolved and carried away.

This leaves a hole in the stone that keeps the same shape as the bone that it once held. As more water seeps into the stone, minerals are deposited in the spaces, creating a cast of the skeleton. It is these casts that we call fossils. Although they are the same size and shape of the bones and look like bones, fossils are not actually bone.

While fossils can tell us a lot about the animals and plants that once lived, the process of fossilization removes pretty much any trace of organic material, such as cells. This means no DNA, because it disappeared millions of years before scientists could get there to keep it safe.

Unfortunately, fossils aren't going to help us clone a dinosaur, but this isn't necessarily the end of any chance to bring back extinct animals. In the *Jurassic Park* franchise, scientists didn't use fossils to resurrect the dinosaurs. They used dinosaur DNA from a completely different place—inside the stomachs of ancient mosquitos trapped inside amber.

Creatures trapped in amber are beautifully preserved specimens ready for eager scientists to unlock their secrets.

DINOSAURS FROM AMBER?

Amber is tree sap, a substance sticky enough to trap insects and even small animals as it slowly flows from trees. The sap hardens into a shiny, sometimes transparent mass that allows whatever might be stuck inside to be seen. On very rare occasions, prehistoric creatures are found inside amber, protected for millions of years from the effects of air and moisture.

In the fictional *Jurassic Park* world, scientists find fragments of dinosaur DNA locked inside amber by drilling into and extracting a preserved mosquito whose last meal was dinosaur blood. Once they find the DNA, the scientists are able to put it back together and fill in missing parts by using DNA from amphibians. With a complete genome, they're able to start building dinosaurs from scratch, including the terrible Tyrannosaurus rex and the intelligent but deadly velociraptor.

In the 1990s, real scientists tried just such a method, and were unable to find any intact dinosaur DNA—or any DNA at all—from insects trapped in amber. They hadn't really expected to. Why not? DNA is extremely fragile. While the cell is alive, DNA is constantly checked and repaired to keep the cell functioning correctly. If it's not cared for, DNA can cause changes to the cell that can hurt the entire organism.

When a plant or animal dies, its body begins to decompose very quickly. The cells making up that creature die, and are unable to keep DNA intact. The genetic material begins to fragment, or break down.

The rate at which DNA decays varies, depending on how the organism dies, but scientists generally think that DNA has a half-life of about 500 years. This means that after about 500 years, half of the genetic material will be un-readable.

DNA AND CANCER?

When a cell reproduces, or divides, mistakes can be made in the copying of DNA. These are sometimes called mutations. Most mutations never harm us. In fact, they are a natural part of life. Usually, cells repair any errors in their genes. Sometimes, if the mutation is extreme enough, the cell can no longer follow the instructions of its genes and can grow out of control. The resulting disease is what we call cancer.

Eventually, all of the DNA breaks down, just as most organic material does. By the time people started to learn what dinosaurs were, their genes were long gone—even those trapped in amber.

[DNA that survives for millions of years just isn't likely.]

Bringing back animals that have been gone for millions of years is very unlikely. We just don't have intact DNA. But the story might be different for more recently extinct animals whose DNA might still be viable. The remains of a well-preserved, un-fossilized animal just might have enough intact DNA to make a clone. One possibility is the woolly mammoth.

WHEN THE MAMMOTHS ROAMED

Extinction is a regular occurrence on Earth. In tracing the fossil record, scientists can see that millions of species have come and gone since life began on this planet. Today, many animals are endangered and facing extinction, and others are already gone. Species such as the passenger pigeon and the Tasmanian tiger have disappeared due to overhunting and loss of habitat caused by humans.

A group of scientists at the Long Now Foundation's revive-and-restore project believe that de-extinction is possible for many kinds of plants and animals. They help to restore sensitive environments and recreate ecosystems as they may have existed years ago. One of their first projects is to bring back the woolly mammoth.

About 10,000 years ago, Earth went through another significant change in its climate—the planet warmed from an ice age. The frozen tundra of North America and Asia was home to steppe bison, saber-toothed cats, and herds of woolly mammoths.

Woolly mammoths were large, standing about 10 feet tall and weighing about 6 tons when fully grown. Adapted for colder environments, they had thick, hairy coats and thick layers of fat that protected them from freezing temperatures.

At that time, creatures better suited for life during an ice age began dying off. Animals that lived in warmer areas moved further north into a warming Arctic, increasing the competition for food and space to live. Just as when the dinosaurs died out, a changing Earth threatened their existence.

[
However, mammoths had to face an additional danger the dinosaurs never had to deal with—humans.
]

Prehistoric hunters preyed upon the large mammals, using them for food, clothing, and even shelter.

The last woolly mammoths disappeared about 4,000 years ago from Wrangel Island, a cold and remote place off the northern coast of Siberia.

FINDING A MAMMOTH

For the most part, remains of woolly mammoths are, like the dinosaurs, fossilized. But not all of them. Recently, inhabitants of Siberia came across remains of animals poking out of the permafrost. These creatures had been hidden and frozen for thousands of years, but are now uncovered due to a warming environment.

At the time of death, these animals were likely covered quickly by mud or water, keeping them away from the open air. The cold climate in which mammoths lived and died provided an excellent opportunity to preserve their bodies and slow the decay of organic material. These are not fossils—some of them are intact animals with bones, teeth, hair, and even organs.

[
Some of these beasts are so well preserved that scientists have even recovered samples of their blood.
]

As the ground begins to thaw and expose these mammoths to moisture, air, and sunlight for the first time in thousands of years, they begin to decompose very quickly. When they are found, scientists rush to the scene to try to preserve them as quickly and carefully as possible. And, sometimes, the efforts pay off. Even though these mammoths have been dead for thousands of years, they are so well preserved that some of their tissue can be recovered by scientists to extract actual mammoth DNA.

WRANGEL ISLAND BEAUTY

Wrangel Island is a place of few humans and many more species of animals than is usual for places in the Arctic region. You can see photographs of this beautiful area at this website.

UNESCO Wrangel Island

GENETICALLY ENGINEERING A WOOLLY MAMMOTH

In order to clone any animal, a complete genome is needed. As we've learned, DNA is so delicate that even well-preserved DNA can become so fragmented that it's unusable. But, sometimes, if they find a DNA fragment large enough to use, scientists can fill in the gaps of the creature's genetic code with a close genetic relative of the deceased animal.

By recovering as many woolly mammoth remains as possible, scientists have the chance to collect lots of woolly mammoth DNA. Then they can look to modern elephants to help rebuild the genome.

Woolly mammoths and Asian elephants last shared a common ancestor between 2.5 and 5 million years ago. As their populations separated, mammoths adapted to colder climates while Asian elephants evolved to live in warmer environments.

Because they are closely related, mammoths and Asian elephants share many similar traits in their DNA. This is extremely helpful for geneticists. Recovered DNA is a bit of a mess—fragments that were once arranged in incredibly long and complex strands are now jumbled together in pieces.

By comparing fragments of woolly mammoth DNA to an intact Asian elephant genome, geneticists can determine where in their DNA the two species are similar, and where they are different. Matching pieces of mammoth DNA to elephant DNA creates a kind of map for a mammoth. And once there's a map, there's a path to follow.

ASSEMBLING THE PUZZLE

Have you ever tried to put together a jigsaw puzzle? Working with fragmented DNA is a little bit like working on a huge puzzle without knowing what the final picture looks like. It helps to know what the picture is before you start assembling the puzzle so you know where the pieces go when you find them. Asian elephants can help geneticists assemble a picture of mammoth DNA in a similar way.

TURNING ELEPHANTS INTO MAMMOTHS

With this mix of mammoth and elephant DNA, scientists aren't trying to build a mammoth genome from scratch. Instead, they are using the blueprint for a woolly mammoth to edit an Asian elephant's DNA to be as much like a mammoth as possible. By removing an unwanted trait from the elephant DNA and replacing it with the desired mammoth trait, a very mammoth-like genome might be constructed. Once completed, cloning would be done in much the same way scientists cloned a sheep to make Dolly—nuclear transfer.

Using an Asian elephant as a surrogate, geneticists, biologists, paleontologists, and the whole world would have to wait between 18 and 22 months for a very mammoth-like animal to be born. Maybe someday, many of these animals could be born and set free.

Would this creature truly be a mammoth? Creating an animal with both mammoth and elephant genes wouldn't be an elephant or a clone of a mammoth. It would be a kind of hybrid, or a combination of two species, with as many mammoth traits as possible.

Scientists also use the process of nuclear transfer to examine complex human diseases and look for treatments.

PLEISTOCENE PARK

The Pleistocene Epoch was a time period that existed from 2.5 million years ago until 11,000 years ago. It was a time of large mammals, such as mammoths and mastodons, as well as woolly rhinoceroses and giant ground sloths. The last ice age occurred during the Pleistocene, and its end marked the extinction of many plants and animals that lived and thrived in a colder environment. Now, a group of people in Siberia is working to re-establish a Pleistocene environment in today's world.

You can look at Pleistocene Park here.

🔍 Pleistocene Park Science Magazine

All animals are born with inherent traits, or instincts. These are things that they simply know how to do without having to be taught. Animals also learn things from their parents and through interactions with other members of their species. Without adult mammoths around to raise and teach this new hybrid animal, it might not be a true woolly mammoth.

Would this mammoth-like baby know how to act and behave like a mammoth? An elephant that is genetically engineered to look like a mammoth might have the physical characteristics necessary to live in a colder environment, but scientists won't really know whether it could learn to survive away from its Asian elephant relatives until one is created and set loose. Fortunately, there's a nature preserve called Pleistocene Park that's ready for when extinct species of the frozen north are brought back to life as hybrids.

Pleistocene Park, named for the Pleistocene Epoch, is a nature preserve in northern Siberia. Its land has been set aside to recreate the environment that once existed there 30,000 years ago.

Russian scientist Sergey Zimov has been working to return a section of the Siberian tundra back to the type of ecosystem that existed when woolly mammoths and woolly rhinos roamed. He believes that bringing large herbivores back to Siberia could help slow climate change and the melting of the permafrost.

By digging for grasses and other plants, large mammals such as horses and bison expose the soil to colder temperatures because they are uncovering ground that is usually insulated by snow and therefore maintaining the permafrost. Returning mammoth-like creatures to the tundra could help protect and preserve a rapidly changing environment.

DE-EXTINCTION AND ETHICS

Bringing back dinosaurs is most likely to remain science fiction, but returning more recently extinct plants and animals is coming closer to science fact. Researchers are working on tools and techniques that will help determine the genome for animals such as the woolly mammoth and the passenger pigeon. Their goal is to provide a way to return very close approximations of these creatures to their former habitats. But is this ethical?

Many species became extinct due to human actions. Some people argue that we have a responsibility to return species to their environment if we can, especially if we were responsible for their decline in the first place. However, many of these habitats have changed. Other plants and animals have filled in the gaps in the ecosystem left behind by these extinct creatures.

The re-introduction of extinct species might have unintended consequences on the environments we have today. What do you think?

You might be able to visit Pleistocene Park someday and see a herd of woolly mammoths lumbering across the grasslands of northern Siberia.

KEY QUESTIONS

- What are some of the benefits to cloning? What are some of the drawbacks?
- What are some of the reasons people are interested in bringing back species that have been extinct for many years?
- What are some of the ethical issues involved in cloning and de-extinction?

MAKE A DOUBLE HELIX

In 1953, James Watson and Frances Crick used models discovered by Rosalind Franklin to determine the chemical structure of DNA—a twisted ladder shape called a double helix. The sides of the ladder are made of sugars and phosphates, while the rungs are made of base pairs. Together, they form the structure that passes genetic information from one generation to the next!

- **Create a model of the structure of DNA.**

  - What type of supplies will you use for the four bases (cytosine, guanine, thymine, and adenine)?

  - How will you attach the pairs together (cytosine goes with guanine, thymine goes with adenine)?

  - How will you create the outside of the ladder structure?

  - How will you set it up to maintain a twist?

To investigate further, consider that if you stretched out a single strand of your DNA, it would reach nearly 6 feet in length. How long would your model need to be to accurately represent the length of a DNA model?

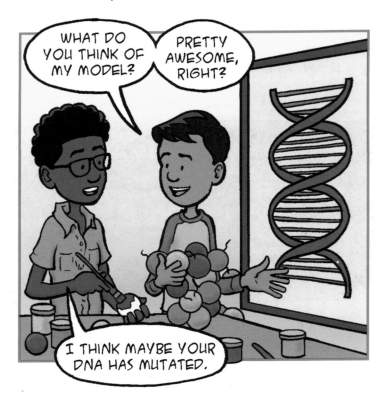

DE-EXTINCTION—YOU CHOOSE

Extinction is part of evolution. Species that are not able to adapt to changes in their environment can disappear from Earth forever. In recent history, humanity has played a larger role in the extinction of species, from overhunting and overfishing to destroying habitats and environments. With the science of de-extinction getting closer to reality, what would you bring back, and why?

- **Do some research and find creatures that are near extinction or recently extinct.** Choose the one you think is the best candidate for de-extinction. Consider the following questions.

  - Why did you choose your animal?

  - When, why, and how did your animal go extinct?

  - Was this extinction caused by humans?

  - What could have been done to avoid its extinction?

  - Does your animal have any close relatives that still exist?

  - Where would this formerly extinct creature live? Does its old habitat still exist?

  - What effects might it have on other species?

- **Print or create a picture of your animal, and include your answers from the questions above to make an infographic.** An infographic combines pictures and information together in a way that is informative and interesting to look at! Don't forget to present and discuss your infographic with others!

VOCAB LAB

Write down what you think each of the following words means. What root words can you find for help?

extinct, **cloning**, **DNA**, **parthenogenesis**, **ethics**, **paleontologist**, **genome**, **mutation**, **half-life**, **permafrost**, and **ethical**.

Compare your definitions with those of your friends or classmates. Did you all come up with the same meanings? Turn to the text and glossary if you need help.

To investigate further, research an endangered species that could go extinct in your lifetime. Answer the same questions and compare and discuss your answers with others.

Inquire & Investigate ▶

Ideas for Supplies ▼

- 3 glasses or clear plastic cups
- bottled water
- salt
- clear dish detergent
- cold isopropyl alcohol
- blue food coloring

To investigate more, consider that your sample contains not only your cells, but the cells of bacteria that live naturally in your mouth. These bacteria cells contain DNA too! What would this mean for a scientist trying to learn about you from this DNA? To extract DNA from other things, check out these experiments.

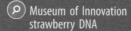

🔍 Museum of Innovation strawberry DNA

EXTRACT YOUR OWN DNA

In the movie *Jurassic Park*, biologists extract dinosaur DNA from mosquito-like bugs that were preserved for millions of years in amber. Today's scientists have not yet turned this fiction into fact, but you can easily see your own DNA in your own home.

- **In a clear cup, stir 2 cups of bottled water with 1 tablespoon of salt until the salt is dissolved.**

- **Place 3 tablespoons of saltwater mixture into a separate cup.** Swish the salt water around in your mouth for 1 minute. Don't swallow it! Spit the saltwater mixture into the second cup. Your cheek cells are now mixed with the salt water.

- **Add a drop of clear dish detergent to the salty cheek water and gently stir it.** This breaks down the cells and releases the DNA. Be careful not to make bubbles!

- **In the third cup, mix ½ cup of isopropyl alcohol and three drops of food coloring.** Pour this mixture into the salty cheek water slowly and gently so that the alcohol crates a layer on top of the salt water. Tip the cups a little as you pour.

- **Wait about 2½ minutes.** Watch for small white clumps and strings forming. This is DNA! DNA is tiny. One million threads of DNA can fit into the dot at the bottom of this exclamation mark!

- **If you need help, watch this short video on the process.**

 🔍 NOVA extract own DNA

Chapter 2

Robots, Androids, and Artificial Intelligence

Can robots and androids ever be similar enough to humans that they can replace us in society?

Robots play major roles in science fiction books and movies, and they are becoming more common in the real world, too.

In science fiction stories, robots can be both heroes and villains. There are the Cylons in *Battlestar Galactica* that want to destroy the human race, and there is *Star Trek*'s android, Data, that wishes he were more human. Science fiction robots often have superhuman abilities—they're able to move faster and go further into dangerous environments and are generally superior to their human counterparts in every way.

Actual robots are far less advanced than those you read about in stories or see in movies, but they still do amazing things, such as building vehicles on assembly lines and disarming explosives in war zones. Real robots are also exploring the solar system, helping doctors perform surgery, and driving humans around in cars.

With robots having this many capabilities, how can we tell what, exactly, is a robot? And are these robots dangerous?

WHAT IS A ROBOT?

Most roboticists define a robot as a machine designed by people to perform a task. Robots gather information from their surroundings, analyze the information, and pick the best way to accomplish their assigned task. This means robots generally have three traits.

- **Sense**: Anything that allows a robot to learn about its surroundings is called a sensor.

- **Thought**: A robot processes information from its sensors through its computer to make a decision.

- **Action**: Once the robot has processed its sensory data, it executes a program by sending signals to effectors.

Sensors can be anything that tells a robot about its environment. Just like our own senses of sight, sound, smell, touch, and taste, robots use cameras, microphones, and pressure sensors to collect similar information about the environment.

> Robots can also use senses we don't have, such as infrared sensors and radar, to collect information that we can't detect.

These sensors send that information to the robot's brain, which is its internal computer. The computer's programming then processes that sensory information to come to conclusions based on the task it was designed to do. The robot's computer brain uses programs created by computer scientists or roboticists to help it determine what to do next.

SCI-FI FACT

The term "robot" was first used by Czech playwright Karel Capek in his 1921 play called *Rossum's Universal Robots*. The word comes from the Czech word *robota*, meaning "hard labor."

ROBOT HALL OF FAME

Did you know there's a Robot Hall of Fame? Robots of science, industry, and science fiction are celebrated in this unique celebration of robot heritage. Check out the page of a robot named Unimate!

🔍 Robot Hall of Fame Unimate

Finally, the robot uses its effectors to take action and perform its set task. Effectors are the parts of a robot that interact with its environment in some way. These can be as simple as lights that turn on and off or as complex as a delicate arm that performs surgery in the operating room. The robots that perform such different tasks won't be the same.

WHAT DO ROBOTS LOOK LIKE?

The first robot to work on an assembly line was called Unimate. Designed as an industrial robot, Unimate's job was to weld automobile parts, sparing humans from doing this difficult and dangerous work.

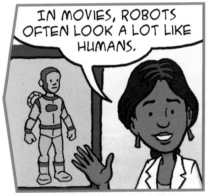

Having machines that were able to work for long periods without tiring or needing a break made a large impact on the automobile industry. Unimate consisted of a single arm, making it simple compared to today's advanced industrial robots, but in the 1960s, it was revolutionary.

Today's industrial robots can work very quickly and do a number of complicated tasks with very little oversight from humans. They can also work safely with materials that are too dangerous for people to handle, such as hazardous waste and dangerous chemicals.

Because of these advantages, humans have kept building better robots to do more jobs. Now robots are able to explore dangerous environments, assemble complicated machines and electronics, and study the solar system in places where humans can't go yet, such as Mars.

ROBOTS THAT EXPLORE

Besides caring for people and doing dangerous work, robots also explore places that are hard to get to, too dangerous, or too far away for humans to attempt. On Earth, scientists use specially designed robots to investigate inside volcanoes, handle explosives, and explore the depths of the ocean. Some robots even travel to other worlds.

The Mars Science Laboratory, better known as the *Curiosity* rover, is the latest robot sent to explore the red planet. It's designed to handle the harsh conditions of the surface of Mars, including extreme cold, radiation, and intense dust storms.

Curiosity was built by scientists who knew about the environment on Mars, but the rover still has to understand its surroundings. To do this, it uses many different kinds of sensors to analyze rocks, soil, and atmosphere on Mars. Using its navigational cameras, or NAVCAM, the car-sized robot looks at its surroundings. Its navigation program uses that information to determine the best way to get to its next location, after checking with its drivers on Earth. *Curiosity*'s six wheels can adjust their speed and direction depending on the type of surface they travel over, making for a slow but steady pace.

ROBOTS THAT HELP HUMANS

In the movie *Big Hero 6*, the robot Baymax is designed to help and care for others. He's programmed with medical knowledge, and tries to help the sick and injured whenever he can. Although Baymax is science fiction, the idea of a robot designed to help and care for humans is not. A Japanese robot called ROBEAR is designed to assist people who can't move themselves. It's a robot programed to be strong but gentle. Made of a soft material, it uses tactile sensors to make sure it never applies too much force when lifting or moving someone.

Watch ROBEAR in action here.

 ROBEAR video

> *Curiosity* is capable of working on Mars for years without a break, though it still depends on roboticists and engineers to provide new programming and future targets for its scientific instruments.

As good as planetary rovers are, they are still limited. Robots are usually designed for one specific set of tasks. Vacuuming robots are short and small so they can easily clean under and around couches and tables. Assembly-line robots are large and able to lift extremely heavy objects. Trying to get robots to do something they're not programmed for simply won't work.

While a robot can use its tools to collect data, it can't make difficult decisions about what to do with that data. A human explorer, on the other hand, can do all sorts of things. For example, a person with geological training can pick up a rock, examine it, and decide what to do next with an important sample. Today's robots can only make a few decisions on their own. They rely on humans to guide them, and humans do this through new programming.

The rover *Curiosity* can't make discoveries on its own. However, science fiction often features robots that are remarkably human-like. These humanoid machines are called androids.

SCI-FI ANDROIDS

In *Star Wars*, C-3PO is designed for "human-cyborg relations" and claims to speak more than 6 million languages. He's made to look and act more like a person than a machine so that people have an easier time interacting with him. Data from *Star Trek: The Next Generation* looks even more human than C-3PO, but isn't able to feel emotions like his fellow crew members aboard the starship *Enterprise*. You can hear Data explain his view of friendship here.

🔍 Data defines friendship

ANDROIDS

Androids are robots designed to look and act like humans. They can walk and talk, but can also do things only machines can do. They might have incredible strength or speak dozens of languages. They could have an incredible number of facts and figures at their robotic fingertips.

Creating an android is not an easy task. From the moment humans are born, we begin learning about the world around us. We grow up surrounded by language, people, and objects, and we learn to communicate ideas in complicated ways. These things become so natural that we don't think about how many systems we use just to ask a question or walk across a room.

Language requires a great understanding of rules and memorization. Walking requires balance and fine control of our motor skills. What would it be like to grow up without any human interaction? Would you have the same skills and abilities? Programming a robot to do all the things that are second nature to humans is extremely difficult.

The human gait is a hard thing for a robot to copy. When we take a step, our brains rely on our sight, touch, and balance to gather information. Our brains process that data and tell our legs and feet what to do next. We're able to avoid obstacles, climb over rocks, and avoid slipping when walking down a slope, all without thinking about it. We can even regain our balance if we feel ourselves starting to fall. Moving is so natural to us that we can hike rocky terrain while talking with our friends.

When we move, we don't think, "left foot up, left foot down," every time we take a step, but this is exactly what a robot's program must do for it to take a step. It must also survey its surroundings, identify hazards, and sense slopes or variations in the terrain.

Humans learn this at a young age, but it still takes many months before we're able to take our first steps. Robots, however, don't get a chance to grow up. We want them to perform immediately and overcome challenges right away.

The rover *Curiosity* serves as a tool for scientists back on Earth.

ATLAS

Boston Dynamics's robot Atlas is able to walk, open doors, stack boxes, and even right itself. Does this android seem human to you?

🔍 Boston Dynamics Atlas

MAY THE BEST ROBOT WIN

So if programming a robot to walk is so difficult, why create a humanoid robot in the first place? Can't we just give it wheels?

Imagine if a robot could drive, climb a ladder, open a door, and carry a human. A robot capable of this would need to be able to function in a human environment, just as a human would. A robot able to do so could rescue people from a burning building without a fireman having to risk his own life, for example.

The Defense Advanced Research Projects Agency (DARPA) Robotics Challenge is a competition to create robots that can perform search-and-rescue operations in disaster situations. Teams from all over the world design machines to perform tasks that are usually easy for human rescuers but extremely difficult for even the most sophisticated robots. During the finals of the 2015 competition, robots were given tasks to accomplish with as little help as possible from their creators. Their creators had to build and program them to drive a car, climb a ladder, and cut through a wall, among other things. The results weren't great.

[In fact, one of the most popular things to come out of the competition was the sight of humanoid robots repeatedly falling down!]

The robots had trouble with many of the tasks because creating a program that can do that many different things well is extremely difficult. Many robots were unable to get up after falling down, something humans learn to do at a very early age. Unfortunately, realistic human motion remains out of reach at the moment, but roboticists are making progress.

Why can't robots learn like us? Humans have intelligence—the ability to learn, think, and act based on our own experiences. To create a truly human-like robot, or android, robots need a kind of intelligence that lets them think and learn on their own. This is called artificial intelligence.

ARTIFICIAL INTELLIGENCE

Artificial intelligence, or AI, plays a major role in science fiction. It's what gives androids their ability to think and act without being given a command. And, just as with people, what and how they learn affects how they behave. Robots such as Disney's WALL-E are capable of thinking and learning in much the same way we do, and they are able to act independently of humans. But it's easier said than done.

Programming a computer to behave like a person has been a goal of computer scientists for many decades. The problem is that even some of the most basic things we can do are still very hard for computers. They are getting better, though, even at playing challenging games.

Previously, computers were able to beat humans at games such as chess simply by calculating millions of moves per second and choosing the best one.

THE COMPUTER THAT PLAYS GO

Go is an ancient and complex Chinese game, said to be many times more difficult to learn and play than chess. In 2016, an artificial intelligence named AlphaGO was the first machine to defeat a human player. In a best of three matches, AlphaGo won the first three games in a row before the human player got their first win. Check out more about Go and AlphaGO here.

 computer mastered Go

In the popular television game show *Jeopardy!*, the host gives contestants answers to clues and they play the game by asking the question that the answer was for. It's a game that requires players to be knowledgeable in a wide array of topics, such as history, art, and science. Players must also have a strong enough understanding of the English language to recognize clues constructed as riddles. Often, the clues use jokes and puns that can stump even the best players. *Jeopardy!* is a challenging game.

A company called IBM created a computer program named Watson to play *Jeopardy!*, making it the first computer that could understand details of English speech as well as access immense amounts of information. In 2011, Watson defeated contestant Ken Jennings to become the first artificial intelligence to be crowned a *Jeopardy!* champion. It was a significant triumph for AI.

> Watson's victory on *Jeopardy!* was the first time a computer was able to understand and interpret complex human language and use it to arrive at the right result faster than a human competitor.

Watson is an example of an artificial intelligence, one that can learn and understand complicated things on its own with little input from programmers and engineers. It can identify patterns in unorganized data such as news articles and books to find connections. This is similar to what your brain does—our brains look for and identify patterns in the world around us.

Computers like Watson are now used by businesses and universities to analyze large amounts of data, study disease, and even answer phone calls. You might be talking to a version of Watson without knowing it!

CHATBOTS AND THE TURING TEST

As good as artificial intelligence systems are getting, they're still a long way from matching their human counterparts. But how can we tell when an AI can really think and act like a human? Could an AI be built that could fool us into thinking it was a person?

We interact through technology every day. We send emails and text messages through computers and cell phones and we know there's a human receiving our emails and messages. But if you were actually having a conversation with a robot, would you be able to tell the difference?

In 1950, computer scientist Alan Turing (1912–1954) developed a test to check if a computer was capable of conversing like a human. During the test, human judges carry on text conversations with different entities and try to determine which are machines and which are humans. If a computer successfully convinces the judges multiple times that it is a human, it is said to have passed the Turing Test. To determine which is the computer and which is human, judges might ask any kind of question they like.

Most of the competitors are chatbots, programs designed to talk with people in as realistic a way as possible. Most chatbots are unable to keep up with the shifting topics and changing questions typical of conversations between people. Eventually, they make a mistake that gives them away as a computer program.

So far, no program has successfully passed the test. But computer scientists are optimistic that an AI will be able to interact seamlessly with humans before too long. So what happens if we create an artificial intelligence as smart as we are, or smarter?

SCI-FI FACT

Alan Turing was a British mathematician and cryptographer who cracked some of the most difficult codes used by the German Army during World War II.

STEPHEN HAWKING, THEORETICAL PHYSICIST

Stephen Hawking (1942–) is considered one of the greatest physicists of all time. His ideas have revolutionized how we see the universe. Professor Hawking suffers from amyotrophic lateral sclerosis (ALS), which affects his muscles and nerves but has left his mind untouched. To interact with the world, he relies on a form of artificial intelligence to help him speak. You can listen to Hawking give a TED talk here.

 Stephen Hawking TED

THE EVIL MACHINES

In *2001: A Space Odyssey*, HAL is an important member of a crew on a journey to study Jupiter and its moons. He is also the onboard computer system. He manages the ship's functions, monitors communication, and plays chess with the crew. He even gives interviews to reporters on Earth, answering questions in a clear, calm voice. Unless you could see that he was a machine, you might easily mistake him for a human.

Unfortunately for the crew, Hal also displays some less desirable traits, such as telling lies and even physically harming the crew. Is artificial intelligence something we should fear?

When scientists design artificial intelligence systems, they do it to better the lives of humans. But how can we control what our sentient computers or robots do when they can learn and do things as well as us, or better?

A few scientists have discussed the possibility that artificial intelligence might overtake and surpass humanity with disastrous results. Stephen Hawking has said that an AI that is capable of learning and evolving on its own could quickly find humans to be more of a problem than help.

In the 1950s, science fiction writer Isaac Asimov thought of this and developed a set of laws to govern the behavior of intelligent robots to ensure that they could never harm a human or humanity. In his series *I, Robot*, Asimov tells stories of a world in which intelligent robots are a part of society, with many reaching the levels of human intelligence. In these tales, Asimov introduces the Laws of Robotics.

These laws were created to guide a robot's behavior and interactions with humans and ensure that they could never knowingly harm a human being.

- **Law 1**: A robot may not injure a human being or, through inaction, allow a human being to come to harm.

- **Law 2**: A robot must obey orders given it by human beings except where such orders would conflict with the First Law.

- **Law 3**: A robot must protect its own existence as long as such protection does not conflict with the First or Second Law.

Later, Asimov added a fourth law, designed to protect humanity as a whole, not just people in general.

- **Law 4**: A robot may not harm humanity or, by inaction, allow humanity to come to harm.

In Asimov's stories, every robot is programmed to know and obey these laws at all times. While the laws can't be changed or erased, interesting ways of testing them make for excellent storytelling. But these laws are not part of modern robots' programming.

Currently, robots are not at the level where these laws might influence their behavior—robots are still firmly under the direction of humans. Robot aerial drones are often used by the military to fight enemies, and people can be harmed in the process. This would violate Asimov's first law of robotics.

ISAAC ASIMOV, GIANT OF SCI-FI

Isaac Asimov is considered one of the masters of science fiction. As a professor of biochemistry at Boston University, he was also an accomplished scientist. His many stories influenced generations of science fiction writers and scientists alike. You can listen to his story, "Robot Dreams."

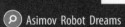 Asimov Robot Dreams

In the *Terminator* movies, self-aware machines rise up against their human creators and try to take control of the planet.

Some well-known scientists and inventors have warned that AI is a threat to humanity. Physicist Stephen Hawking believes that sentient machines could become more intelligent than humans and ultimately find us a threat to their existence. Inventor and entrepreneur Elon Musk agrees, believing there should be some kind of regulation to oversee the development of artificial intelligence systems. Other scientists disagree, and trust that artificial intelligence will change the world in positive ways, such as helping to solve climate change problems or cure cancer.

Science fiction gives us a place to examine a wide array of possibilities and discuss the good things and the bad so we can think through a technology before building it. But for the moment, we're still a long way from having a self-aware AI or robots capable of interacting with the world the way people do. If robots and androids are ever capable of learning and acting like humans, they'll need guidance and instruction just as we do to live and function in our society.

KEY QUESTIONS

- Why is it difficult to design and program robots to behave like humans?

- What kinds of problems do you think artificial intelligence could help solve?

- Do you think robots could be dangerous for humans?

CHATTING WITH CHATBOTS

The Turing Test is designed to see if a computer program can convince a human that they're talking to another human. Many computer scientists have created chatbots and tried to pass the Turing Test with programs that are designed to respond to questions and conversations like humans. The first chatbot, ELIZA, was developed in the 1960s. Since then, many chatbots have been created, but none have officially passed the Turing Test. What's it like to talk with a chatbot?

- **There are many chatbots, but two of the most well-known are A.L.I.C.E and Cleverbot.** Which responds more like a person? Can you stump a chatbot? Can they fool your friends?

  A.L.I.C.E · Cleverbot

- **Prepare a questionnaire and ask the chatbot your questions.**

  - What will you ask?

  - Will you ask about themselves, the world, or something else?

  - How do they respond to each questions?

  - How are their responses similar or different?

  - Could you be fooled into thinking they are real people?

  - What gives them away as computer programs?

> To investigate further, ask a friend to answer the same questions you asked the chatbots, and record their answers. Next, ask another friend to try to determine which responses are from chatbots and which are from a human. Do a chatbot's responses fool anyone? How could you increase the chances of someone being fooled by a chatbot?

DESIGN YOUR OWN ROBOT

Most robots are designed to do specific tasks. If you could design your own robot, what kinds of tasks would you like it to do? Would you like it to help with chores around the house, explore the surface of Mars, or be your best friend?

- **Define a purpose.** What do you want your robot to do?

- **Give it sensors.** How will your robot learn about the world around it? Will it need cameras, pressure sensors, or to be able to hear? Think about what your robot will need to be able to accomplish its tasks. Will the sensors help the robot do what it's designed to do?

- **Give it a brain.** How smart will your robot be? Will it be able to respond to human commands? Will you be in charge of most of its movements, or will it be able to make decisions on its own? How many things will it be capable of doing?

- **Let it work.** How will your robot interact with the world? What kind of effectors will your robot have? Will it need arms, legs, or wheels to get around? Does it need to lift or move anything? Think about its task and make sure it can accomplish its job!

- **Design the look of your robot.** Using art supplies, a computer program, or anything you like, design your robot. What will it look like? How big or small will it be? Will it be humanoid?

To investigate further, build your own robot. There are many kits and programs to help you get started in robotics. Check out a few below! Can you build the robot you designed?

🔍 Lego MINDSTORMS · VEX Robotics · Little Bits

Chapter 3 ▶
Living on Mars

Why are humans interested in living on the Red Planet?

Inhabiting another planet has long been a human dream, and Mars is the planet that has the most potential of being habitable.

Science fiction makes living on other planets look easy. Most books and movies present alien worlds as Earth-like, though they might host exotic life forms, have weaker gravity, or orbit two suns. Even Mars is usually shown as much more Earth-like than it really is. But the movie *The Martian* is a little different from most stories about Mars. It shows the planet as a hostile, difficult place for humans to live, especially if you're a botanist stranded alone with little hope of being rescued.

The Martian is among the most realistic examples of just how hard getting to and living on Mars will be for future astronauts. The story uses a lot of real science and technology that isn't too futuristic. Right now, scientists and engineers are working to develop the necessary technologies to get humans to Mars in the 2030s. Many agree this is just the first step toward making humanity a truly multi-planetary species.

THE EARTH AND MARS

Earth is a special place. From microbes and mosquitos to whooping cranes and whales, it's the only planet we know of that can support life. Everything that thrives on Earth has evolved and adapted to this planet, with its thick, oxygen-rich atmosphere, plenty of water, and sunlight. Life is protected from deadly radiation by the planet's strong magnetic field and atmosphere. Earth orbits at just the right distance from the sun to have an average surface temperature of 57 degrees Fahrenheit. The conditions on Earth are perfect.

Mars is both similar and very different. Orbiting about 1.5 times as far from the sun, a year on Mars lasts 687 Earth days. A Martian day, or sol, is only 37 minutes longer than a day on Earth. Both planets have icecaps, mountains, canyons, and volcanoes.

> Mars is the most Earth-like planet we know, but there are differences between Earth and Mars that are more important for life on these planets.

Being farther from the sun, Mars receives less solar energy. It's cold! The average surface temperature is -51 degrees Fahrenheit, quite a bit colder than most places on Earth. Mars also lacks a protective magnetic field, allowing radiation from space to reach the ground. What little atmosphere remains on Mars is about 100 times thinner than ours and is made mostly of carbon dioxide.

SCI-FI FACT

Scientists and meteorite hunters sometimes find meteorites from Mars here on Earth!

GRAVITY ON MARS

With a diameter of just 2,110 miles, Mars is only half as wide as Earth. It's also only 15 percent as massive, meaning the pull of gravity is much weaker. Standing on the surface of Mars, you would weigh only about one-third of your weight on Earth!

All of these factors mean there are no oceans, lakes, or rivers on the surface of Mars. Even so, it's possible for humans to live there, if we have the right technology. But before we can think of living on Mars, we have to get there.

THE PATH TO MARS

The trip to Mars will be a long and dangerous one. So far, human exploration of space has relied on chemical propulsion, which is powerful enough to lift people and supplies off Earth but not very good at letting us travel between planets. In 1968, it took three days for *Apollo 8* to travel to the moon and another three days for the crew to get back home—a 480,000-mile round trip took nearly a week.

Mars, at its closest, is about 40 million miles away. A voyage there will take months using even our most powerful rocket engines.

[
To make the trip to Mars even more difficult, there are no straight lines when traveling from one planet to another.
]

All the planets in the solar system orbit the sun, and any spacecraft that travels between planets will do the same. To travel from Earth to Mars, a spacecraft needs to plan its trajectory so that its orbit intercepts the orbit of Mars at just the right place and time.

Because the distances between Earth and Mars are always changing, planning the shortest path to Mars is important. The longer the voyage, the more the astronauts are exposed to the dangers of space.

The amount of time and energy needed to travel from Earth to Mars is at its lowest every 26 months. This is called a launch window.

In the next chapter, we'll look at how the speed of light will further affect our ability to travel to Mars.

SPACE TRAVEL CHALLENGES

Science fiction stories often describe large and roomy ships. These come with private rooms, fresh food, running water, large viewing windows, and Earth-like gravity.

The reality of space travel is very different. Spacecraft designed to lift astronauts to the International Space Station tend to be compact, with just enough room to give astronauts a safe ride to orbit. Any craft designed to take humans from Earth to Mars will need to be larger, more comfortable, and capable of protecting passengers from the dangers of deep space.

One of the greatest dangers to people in space is radiation. The radiation in space is different from the radiation we experience here at home. Earth's magnetic field and substantial atmosphere help block most harmful radiation rays from reaching the surface. For astronauts, cosmic radiation, also called cosmic rays, are extremely harmful and difficult to protect against.

Some cosmic rays come from our sun as particles emitted during solar flares. These particles move at extremely high speeds and have enough energy to easily penetrate the thin metal walls of space habitats. They have an impact on astronauts' bodies. When cosmic particles enter cells in the body, they can damage them. This can lead to problems such as cataracts and cancer.

Other cosmic rays, called galactic cosmic rays, come from outside the solar system. They zip through the galaxy at nearly the speed of light and cause the same kind of damage.

Scientists are studying ways to shield astronauts from this deadly radiation. Certain materials, such as water and even human waste, can absorb or deflect these harmful rays. But radiation isn't the only challenge.

The most common forms of harmful radiation we experience on Earth are ultraviolet rays and X-rays. Ultraviolet rays are emitted by the sun and are what cause sunburns. Most of our exposure to X-rays is from visits to the doctor!

THE GRAVITY OF THE SITUATION

The longer the journey, the more important it is for astronauts to stay strong.

On Earth, we are held to the ground by the force of gravity. Our bones and muscles fight against this force to stand, jump, and move around, keeping us in good shape. In space, astronauts are in a microgravity environment, or weightlessness, for long periods of time.

When our bodies are no longer fighting the force of gravity, strange things begin to happen. Muscles don't need to work as hard, so they shrink from disuse, leaving them weaker. Bones lose density, making them more brittle. Even the fluids in our bodies behave differently in microgravity. On Earth, blood, water, and other fluids are pumped upwards to the heart and brain against gravity's pull. Without this force, astronaut's bodies overcompensate, giving them a puffy or bloated look. This can be uncomfortable!

To counteract the effects of muscle and bone loss, astronauts spend hours every day exercising on special machines. On the International Space Station (ISS), they have a treadmill with straps to hold runners in place, simulating the force of gravity. These are important tools to keep bodies healthy so astronauts can walk when they return to Earth. The same kinds of measures will be used to make sure astronauts will be strong enough to move around on Mars.

Some science fiction stories solve the weightlessness problem by creating artificial gravity, holding space travelers firmly in place with special gravity plating or gravity fields. Is there a way to create gravity within a spacecraft? There is, but not the way it's done on television.

SCI-FI FACT

Watch NASA astronaut Karen Nyberg demonstrate the fitness machines in use aboard the International Space Station.

🔍 space station treadmill

Try holding a can of soda in each hand with your arms outstretched, and then pull them in to your chest. Now try the same thing, but while spinning very fast.

Was it harder to pull the cans to your chest while spinning or standing still? When you're spinning, your arms experience centripetal force, which pushes your arms away from your body as you turn. Anything inside a spinning object would feel a force away from the center of rotation, and this can simulate the pull of gravity.

[
If astronauts could experience centripetal force in a rotating space ship, it would feel like gravity holding them to the floor of the ship.
]

In the 1968 movie *2001: A Space Odyssey*, the inside of Space Station V looked a lot like a nice hotel on Earth. Travelers experienced gravity because of its spinning wheel shape. However, producing this kind of artificial gravity is not easy.

Exercise isn't the only thing astronauts will need on a trip to Mars. In addition to keeping bones and muscles in good form, astronauts will need to eat a balanced diet.

WHAT ARE YOU DOING? I'M GETTING DIZZY JUST WATCHING YOU!

I'M TRAINING TO BE AN ASTRONAUT!

INTERPLANETARY SPACE CRAFT WILL SPIN TO SIMULATE GRAVITY.

I'M GETTING USED TO THE CENTRIPETAL FORCE.

YOU KNOW, YOU WON'T ACTUALLY BE ABLE TO FEEL THE SHIP SPINNING?

THAT'S A RELIEF BECAUSE I WAS ABOUT TO BE SICK!

On the International Space Station, even some urine is recycled.

Imagine a spacecraft as a giant spinning wheel, with inhabitants working and living on the outer rim. The amount of centripetal force depends on the diameter of the wheel and its rate of spin. The smaller the wheel, the faster it has to spin to generate the same force as a large wheel spinning more slowly. But a wheel with a small diameter could be very disorienting to astronauts. Because centripetal force increases the farther you are from the center of the wheel, the astronaut's feet could experience a greater force than their head, drawing blood away from their brains. This might cause them to lose consciousness!

The bigger the wheel, the less difference in force between an astronaut's head and their feet, making it a more comfortable situation. A large spinning structure on a spaceship would be very complicated and heavy, though. These are two things to avoid on a spacecraft traveling millions of miles from Earth to Mars.

NASA has experimented with centrifuges to see if small amounts of centripetal force can help astronauts counter some effects of microgravity. Because the first humans to journey to Mars will want to be able to walk on the surface when they arrive, it will be extremely important that they stay fit and healthy on the journey.

PACKING FOR A TRIP TO MARS

Astronauts on the ISS rely on regular resupply missions from Earth for meals, including some fresh food. Astronauts going to Mars will have to take everything with them.

The food of the early space programs was mostly unappetizing freeze-dried or dehydrated packages. One of the main reasons for this was to eliminate crumbs that could clog instruments or ruin experiments. Modern space meals have gotten much better.

Astronauts today have dozens of choices on a typical space station menu.

On a voyage to Mars, astronauts will need to use both prepackaged and grown food. However, food and water can be very heavy things to carry. Careful use and recycling of water will be essential to keeping a crew alive and healthy during the months-long trip. Explorers will need more than just drinking water—they'll also need water to conduct experiments and grow food on the way. Once they reach Mars, they might have more options.

[Mars has plenty of water, but getting to it and making it potable won't be easy.]

Most of the water on Mars lies frozen deep underground. To use it, astronauts will need to bring it to the surface. However, the water on Mars is thought to be much saltier than Earth's oceans, so astronauts will need to remove the salt to make it drinkable. On Earth, this is done to turn seawater into fresh drinking water. It takes a lot of time and energy, but it's possible. Having fresh Martian water would make living on the planet much easier.

FARMING ON MARS

Based on what scientists have learned about Martian soil from previous missions, growing plants on Mars is possible with a little help from Earth. NASA has developed a simulated Mars soil to test different growing techniques, and scientists have found that adding just a little organic material from Earth can provide enough of a boost to get plants growing. Plants would need to be grown inside a greenhouse to provide Earth-like pressures and temperatures.

Children could be born and raised on Mars—they might consider themselves the first true Martians!

[
Giving plants close to the same conditions they have on Earth will increase the likelihood of them growing well and feeding hungry astronauts.
]

The surface of Mars might be used for more than farming. Scientists and engineers are investigating ways of using Martian dirt to create habitats and protect astronauts from radiation. It might even be used to make fuel to help with a return trip to Earth.

MARS ON EARTH

To prepare for a long stay on a hostile world, humans need to practice all aspects of living on Mars. This includes growing food and finding water to living with others in a small, confined space. And we can do that much closer to home. The Mauna Loa volcano of Hawaii is a good substitute for Mars. At an altitude of 8,000 feet and with little vegetation, the slope of the giant active volcano does look a lot like the red planet.

Since opening in 2013, the HI-SEAS Mars simulation has provided researchers with important information on what it's like to live in an isolated environment for a long time.

HI-SEAS tests involve crews of six who live and work together on a year-long simulated Mars mission. Just as they would on Mars, the crew spends most of their time living in a small dome that contains living quarters, workspaces, and an airlock.

Participants are only allowed out of the dome to perform experiments on the volcanic slope, and only if they're wearing a spacesuit. These kinds of simulations allow scientists to test new spacesuits and rovers, and also learn what psychological challenges a crew living on Mars might face.

Just like real astronauts, these crews don't get to go home to their families after a long day. They have to live and work with very little personal space and privacy with the same five people for a full year!

LIVING AND DYING ON MARS

While NASA and other space agencies are focused on just getting to Mars and back, others are looking farther into the future. For a longer or permanent stay on Mars, astronauts will have to set up a colony. This would be a way for scientists to study Mars in far more detail. Elon Musk, the founder of the rocket company Space Exploration Technologies (SpaceX), founded his company with the goal of making humanity a two-planet species. He envisions large cities on Mars that will eventually function with no help from Earth. This reality is very far in the future, but it's exciting to think about!

For many, the drive to become a two-planet species comes from the knowledge that we live on a fragile world. Is it possible that humans could face extinction at some point, just as the dinosaurs did millions of years ago? Having a second place to call home could greatly increase humanity's chance of survival.

CLIMATE CHANGE

One reason scientists are interested in finding ways to live on Mars is because climate change is altering the environment on our home planet. Check out the link to learn more about climate change.

PS

climate change

RED TO GREEN(ISH)

TERRAFORMING MARS IN SCIENCE FICTION

The Red Mars series by Kim Stanley Robinson details the effort to change Mars from a cold, dry world into a more Earth-like environment, and all the struggles that could come with it. In the first book, Kim writes: "In games there are rules, but in life the rules keep changing." What do you think this means?

An AU, or astronomical unit, is the average distance from Earth to the sun, about 93 million miles.

Studies of Mars have shown us that the planet was once much more like Earth. Could Mars be made more like Earth today? For Mars to truly be a second home, we'd need to live on the surface as we do on Earth, moving around outside without the need for a spacesuit. To do this, we'd need to engineer the entire planet through a process called terraforming.

At about 1.5 AUs from the sun, Mars receives only about 42 percent of the solar energy received by Earth. Most of this solar energy is lost because the thin atmosphere on Mars can't hold onto it. To start terraforming, we would need to thicken the atmosphere, raising both the temperature and pressure on the surface. There are a few interesting ways to do this.

The first would be to create climate change. A few proposals to make this happen sound more like science fiction than real science. Some scientists suggest painting the poles of Mars with a dark substance, such as charcoal. Since the color black absorbs more energy from the sun than bright white ice, it should be capable of thawing the frozen carbon dioxide, which would move into the atmosphere and thicken it. Others have suggested exploding nuclear bombs above the poles, thawing the carbon dioxide ice and melting the water ice all at once, though this would spread a lot of deadly radiation in the process. A third option is to crash a comet into the surface of the planet, which would make a big mess, but provide water and heat all at once.

These are extreme ideas. There might be a better solution right here on Earth. Scientists have found that releasing greenhouse gases such as carbon dioxide into Earth's atmosphere causes a measurable increase in the average surface temperature.

> Although excess carbon dioxide gas
> is not a good thing for our planet,
> it could be just what Mars needs.

These initial steps toward terraforming would make Mars's surface pressure and temperature slowly increase, so water could exist on the surface as a liquid. Some studies show that once surface pressure reaches a certain level, both the temperature and pressure would be high enough to keep water flowing in many places on Mars during the long summers. At that point, a full spacesuit would no longer be necessary for people on the surface.

AIR TO BREATHE

Making the atmosphere breathable needs a different approach. On Earth, most of the oxygen we breathe is created when plants take in carbon dioxide and produce oxygen. To get to this point on Mars, we need to take a few steps first.

With a thicker, warmer atmosphere, biologists and botanists could start introducing genetically engineered organisms that help condition the Martian soil by removing nitrogen from the atmosphere and putting it into the soil. When the soil is more Earth-like, larger forms of life, such as lichen, mosses, and eventually trees, could be planted. Once established, massive forests could start the process of taking in carbon dioxide and producing oxygen, just as they do on Earth. Imagine what a Martian forest might look like!

Once we colonize Mars, where might we go next? To explore worlds beyond our solar system, we'd need to travel very, very fast to cover the huge distances between stars. Is that even possible?

NEW EARTH

Terraforming Mars can't be done overnight. Scientists estimate it could take anywhere from 100 to 100,000 million years to make Mars as Earth-like as possible, and it still wouldn't be exactly like Earth.

Martian gravity is only one-third the gravity of Earth. Nobody knows what living your whole life in Martian gravity would be like. People born and raised on Mars might never be able to travel to Earth. Their bodies might not be able to adapt to Earth's greater gravity. Martians might eventually evolve into a separate species!

KEY QUESTIONS

- Why is living on Mars such a difficult problem to solve?
- Why is it useful to train in certain places on Earth that are similar to Mars?

COMPARE EARTH, THE MOON, AND MARS

From Earth, the moon can sometimes look incredibly close. Even without a telescope, we can see its volcanic plains and mountainous highlands. In 1969, *Apollo 11* took a little more than three days to travel to the moon, and about the same amount of time to come back. But a journey to Mars will take much, much longer because it is incredibly far away. At its closest, Mars is almost 40 million miles from Earth, and appears as a bright, reddish star in the sky. Creating scale models of the Earth, the moon, and Mars can help us understand the distances in the solar system.

- **Make a model Earth.** Balloons are a good material to use. Blow up a balloon until it's about 8 inches in diameter and tie it off. This is Earth!

- **Find the scale size for the moon and Mars.** If the model of Earth is 8 inches in diameter, how big should the moon and Mars be? To find the scale factor, divide the diameter of Earth by the model diameter. To find the diameter of the Mars and moon models, divide their actual diameters by the scale factor. You might find a table like the one below helpful.

BODY	DIAMETER (MILES)	MODEL DIAMETER (INCHES)
Earth	7,926	8
Moon	2,159	
Mars	4,222	

VOCAB LAB 📖

Write down what you think each of the following words means. What root words can you find for help?

microbe, **cosmic radiation**, **microgravity**, **centripetal force**, **centrifuge**, and **potable**.

Compare your definitions with those of your friends or classmates. Did you all come up with the same meanings? Turn to the text and glossary if you need help.

- **Make models of the moon and Mars with the correct diameters.** Which is the largest?

- **Model the distances between Earth and the moon and Earth and Mars.** The shortest distance from Earth to the moon is 238,606 miles. What would be the distance between the model Earth and moon? Use the scale factor you found earlier to calculate the model distance from Earth to the moon and from Earth to Mars.

BODIES	SHORTEST DISTANCE (MILES)	MODEL DISTANCE (INCHES)
Earth to Moon	238,606	20 cm
Earth to Mars	39,767,756	

- Can you make a scale model to show the distances between Earth, the moon, and Mars? Why or why not?

- How long would it take for you to walk the model distance between Earth and the moon? What about the model distance between Earth and Mars?

- What would happen to the model distances if you used smaller models or bigger models?

- How does making a model help you understand the distances between planets?

To investigate further, try calculating the model sizes and model distances for other planets. Can you make the models or model their distances? Mars is 248,548,477 miles from Earth at its farthest distance away. What would the model distance be?

CENTRIPETAL FORCE

In the science fiction classic *2001: A Space Odyssey*, astronauts aboard the spaceship *Discovery* experience a kind of artificial gravity thanks to a large, rotating wheel inside the spaceship. How does it work?

Usually, having an upside-down bucket of water over your head means you'll be getting wet. But what if that bucket of water is moving very quickly in a circular motion? Centripetal force is the inward force that occurs when an object is moving in a circular path. Can you swing the bucket and keep yourself dry?

- **In an open outdoor space, fill a small bucket half full with water.** Tie one end of the rope to the handle of the bucket, and hold the other end of the rope tightly in your hand. You might want to wrap the rope around your hand so it doesn't slip out of your grip.

- **Start by slowly rocking the bucket back and forth.** Gradually build up enough speed to swing the bucket in a vertical circle, having the bucket upside down at the top of its swing.

  - Were you able to keep the water in the bucket? Why or why not?

  - What is happening to the water at the top of its arc? At the bottom?

  - What happens if you try to slow or stop the swing of the bucket?

  - What happens if you let go?

  - How does this compare to a spinning spaceship? What would the bucket represent? What would the water represent?

To investigate further, try the experiment with different lengths of rope. Does it change how you spin the bucket and water?

Chapter 4

Aliens

Why are humans interested in life on other planets?

It's human nature to wonder about life outside our own planet and the possibilities offered by space exploration.

On October 30, 1938, Americans across the country sat by their radios and listened to news of Martians making their way across New Jersey. Reporters breathlessly described the monstrous machines the aliens piloted, causing terror and destruction wherever they went. Horrific scenes captivated listeners who believed they were the Martians' first stop on their way to taking over the world. It would have been terrifying, if it had been true.

The broadcast was a radio adaptation of the classic 1898 novel by H.G. Wells, *The War of the Worlds*. Produced by expert storyteller Orson Welles, the radio broadcast did much more than frighten people with thoughts of an alien invasion. As one of the earliest stories to feature creatures from another world, it inspired both scientists and science fiction writers to wonder if there might be intelligent life beyond Earth.

From *Star Wars* to *Star Trek*, aliens are a huge part of science fiction, but they are also the focus of a lot of real science. Scientists are listening for signals from distant civilizations and robots are digging into Martian soil looking for signs of past or present life. Astronomers are looking at the thousands of exoplanets found orbiting other stars to see if any of them could host life.

Before talking about the ways in which scientists are looking for aliens, we have to look at what makes a world habitable. And if we do find habitable worlds, what are the chances those worlds have intelligent life?

FOLLOW THE WATER

To look for life on other planets, scientists start with what they know—life on Earth. One thing we know about life on our planet is that every form of life needs water to survive. Even in the most extreme environments—at the bottom of the ocean, deep underground, and even in the driest deserts—life can thrive as long as it has access to water.

In the search for alien life, scientists follow the water. If we find water elsewhere in the universe, we just might find life there, too. And we don't have to look that far.

> Our solar system is a wet one, but the problem is that most of this water exists in the form of ice.

The farther we get from the sun, the more ice we find. The moons of the outer planets and even some dwarf planets have large amounts of frozen water on and below the surface. But to find life as we know it, astrobiologists are looking for liquid water.

SCI-FI FACT

Astrobiology is the study of life in the universe. Astrobiologists often study biology, chemistry, geology, and astronomy to understand how and where life might occur.

The first close-ups of Mars, 1965

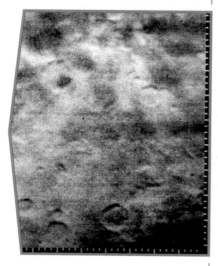

photo credit: NSSDC

WHERE ARE THE MARTIANS?

More than 100 years ago, astronomers using the best telescopes of the time looked at Mars and thought it might be home to alien life. Astronomer Percival Lowell believed he could see canals crisscrossing the Martian surface. He took this as proof that Mars was home to an intelligent civilization that had managed to build a global network of canals to distribute the planet's water evenly to all citizens. He was proved wrong, but even the possibility of water flowing on another world added to people's interest in Mars and the possibility of life beyond Earth.

Hopes of finding Martians began to fade as telescopes became more powerful and astronomers got better views of Mars. On July 14, 1965, the *Mariner 4* probe raced by the planet, sending back the first close-up images. These images crushed hopes of finding evidence of a Martian civilization. The red planet turned out to be a vast, cratered desert. There were no rivers, lakes, or canals, and no ancient Martian civilization.

Scientists were unwilling to give up hope that there might be something alive on the surface of Mars and decided to take an even closer look. In the 1970s, NASA sent twin probes, *Viking 1* and *Viking 2*, to Mars. Their goal was to take photos of the surface, learn about the atmosphere, and search for evidence of life. Each spacecraft consisted of an orbiter to study the planet from above and a lander to investigate the surface.

Viking 1 landed on Mars and sent back the first picture from the surface of another planet on July 20, 1976. The red rocks and soil of the landing site at Chryse Planitia looked a lot like the many deserts on Earth.

> This seemingly familiar landscape gave many people hope that there might be life hiding somewhere on the surface. *Viking 2* followed, landing at Utopia Planitia on September 3.

Neither lander found obvious signs of life. There were no fossils, no ancient ruins, no Martians smiling for the camera. Both landers were equipped with instruments to look for microbes, but found none. The soil was measured and found incapable of supporting the kind of life the *Vikings*'s instruments were designed to detect.

This changed the way scientists approached the search for life on Mars. According to the *Vikings*, Mars wasn't able to support life on its surface now, but scientists thought it might have had the right environment for life in its distant past. Since the *Viking* landers, no mission has specifically looked for life on Mars. Instead, they look for signs that the planet could have developed life in the past.

Chryse Planitia is Latin for "the plains of gold." Utopia Planitia is Latin for "the plains of nowhere."

The first picture from the surface of Mars, July 20, 1976

photo credit: NASA

NASA's Mars exploration rovers *Spirit* and *Opportunity* landed on Mars in 2004. They are a pair of roving robotic geologists that look at the rocks on Mars to find evidence of the planet's ancient environment. NASA's Mars Science Laboratory mission, which landed the rover *Curiosity* on the surface in 2012, studies both the chemistry and geology of Mars to determine the history of the planet's environment. And the news has been good!

[*Curiosity* has found that Mars was once a much warmer and wetter world.]

Images from orbiting spacecraft show ancient riverbeds, lakes, and the shoreline of what could have been a large ocean. It seems that, despite its current dry conditions, Mars might have been much like Earth 3 to 4 billion years ago—warm, wet, and capable of hosting microbial life.

There may be hope for simple life to exist on Mars, buried deep under the Martian soil or somehow living off the traces of salty water.

WAIT, IS THAT RUNNING WATER?

Until recently, most scientists believed that liquid water could not exist on the surface of Mars. For water to exist as a liquid, a planet must have two things: a warm enough temperature to keep it from freezing and a high enough atmospheric pressure to keep it from boiling away.

While Mars is capable of having temperatures as high as 70 degrees Fahrenheit, its thin atmosphere won't let liquid water stick around. The average surface pressure on Mars is 100 times less than what we feel on Earth! At this pressure, water would boil away very quickly.

Many researchers once believed that the low surface pressure made it impossible for water to exist as a liquid on the Martian surface. They were wrong.

NASA's Mars Reconnaissance Orbiter (MRO) made another fascinating discovery in 2015. From orbit, MRO observed dark streaks of soil that came and went with time. They tended to appear mostly in warm seasons and disappear when the weather turned cold.

This is what happens on Earth in northern climates—water thaws in the spring and runs downhill, then freezes again in the winter. By using MRO's spectrometer, a tool that measures the properties of light, scientists determined that these streaks were evidence of hydrated salts called perchlorates.

Perchlorates are able to lower the freezing point of water from 32 degrees Fahrenheit to as low as -94 degrees Fahrenheit. This is important because temperatures can be much warmer than this near the equator during the Martian day. Also, water mixed with perchlorates evaporates more slowly than it would if it was pure, making it possible for small amounts of very salty water to exist on the surface for short periods of time.

[Mars, previously thought to have water only in the form of ice, might actually have the liquid water needed for life!]

Any organism would need to be very tough to survive on Mars, even with the possibility of liquid water. Without a magnetic field or thick atmosphere, the planet's surface is constantly bathed in deadly radiation. Also, the low atmospheric pressure and large changes in temperature don't make for a comfortable home. Still, on planet Earth, biologists have found life in the most unexpected places.

BOILING WATER ON MARS

You might think that boiling water depends only on getting it to the right temperature, but that's not the whole story. The temperature that water boils at depends on the atmospheric pressure, or how hard the air is pressing down on the water. At low pressures, water begins to boil at lower temperatures. On Mars, the surface pressure is so low that water can boil at 50 degrees Fahrenheit! At sea level on Earth, water boils at 212 degrees Fahrenheit.

ATACAMA DESERT, THE DRIEST PLACE ON EARTH

When searching for life on Mars, it helps to find Mars-like places on Earth. Scientists are exploring the incredibly arid climate of the Atacama Desert to learn how organisms cope with such dry conditions, and how that might affect the search for life on Mars. The Atacama Desert once went more than 14 years without a drop of rain! Does this photo look like it could come from Mars?

Chile's Atacama Desert, the driest place on Earth

On Earth, organisms called extremophiles can live in some very harsh conditions. Extremophiles are found in the salty, dry Atacama Desert of Chile, in the frozen permafrost of the Arctic, and even in nuclear waste. There are whole ecosystems on Earth centered around deep-ocean volcanic vents, allowing life forms to thrive without sunlight.

Methanogens are another example of life that's able to survive in extreme locations. Found in hot springs, acidic lakes, and Arctic permafrost, these organisms don't need oxygen or nutrients or even sunlight to survive. All they need is a source of methane. Researchers have tested them in a Martian environment and discovered that they, too, can live in environments with radiation, extreme cold, and low pressure.

[
Astrobiologists believe that extremophiles on Earth show that survival is possible on Mars under the right conditions. Life on Mars might be similar to the extremophiles of Earth.
]

photo credit: European Southern Observatory

While the possibility of microorganisms on Mars might not be as exciting as an ancient Martian civilization, their discovery would raise a lot of interesting questions. How and when did they evolve? Do they have DNA? If so, are they related to organisms here on Earth? Might life on Earth have started on Mars first, traveling here on rocks knocked loose from the red planet in huge meteor impacts? Might we all be Martians?

Some scientists believe this might have happened. Mars, being smaller and farther from the sun, likely cooled earlier than Earth. Giant impacts on Mars, common during the early development of the solar system, might have sent rocks containing Martian organisms on a collision course with our planet. If life was able to start on Mars under just the right conditions, the red planet might have provided Earth with its first organisms.

The discovery of any kind of life on Mars would go beyond Mars itself. It might tell us where we came from, too. While science fiction can explore these ideas, only science fact can give us the answers.

FOLLOWING THE WATER— EUROPA AND ENCELADUS

Mars isn't the only place in the solar system that science fiction imagines hosting life. The movie *Europa Report* follows a group of explorers who travel to Jupiter's moon Europa and encounter something amazing and unexpected beneath its surface. In Arthur Clarke's novel *2010*, a sequel to the movie *2001: A Space Odyssey*, the human race is told by a strange alien intelligence to leave Europa alone. This alien intelligence seems determined to let life evolve on the moon without any interruption from humanity. What makes Europa so interesting to creators of science fiction?

I WILL SURVIVE

One example of an extremophile is the bacteria Deinococcus radiodurans. It can survive in acid and even extreme temperatures. Scientists exposed it to temperatures as low as -110 degrees Fahrenheit and zapped it with radiation to simulate conditions under a foot of Martian soil—it survived. Another example is the Halobacteriaceae family of microbes that are thought to be some of the oldest forms of life on Earth and are known to survive in extremely salty conditions. Biologists discovered that they, too, can survive in a simulated Martian climate of low pressure and extreme cold.

Jupiter's moons Ganymede and Calisto are also suspected to have large underground oceans of water.

The gas giants Jupiter, Saturn, Uranus, and Neptune all have moons, some of which are bigger than the planet Mercury. Two of these moons, Jupiter's Europa and Saturn's Enceladus, stand out from the rest.

[Europa and Enceladus are suspected of having huge oceans beneath their surfaces.]

Both moons have very few craters, which tells scientists that some process keeps erasing any marks and smoothing out their surfaces. Many suspect the resurfacing is due to water pushing up through cracks and spilling over the surface before it freezes, a process that has been going on for thousands or even millions of years.

On Earth, we see this happen with molten rock, or lava, that flows from cracks in the ground as part of a geological process called volcanism. On these moons, ice and water take the place of rocks and lava in a process called cryovolcanism. The idea of Europa and Enceladus having young and changing surfaces has been backed up by images from spacecraft flying by and orbiting these giant planets.

Europa

photo credit: NASA

The *Voyager* and *Galileo* spacecraft returned many spectacular images of Europa that showed its cracked and fractured surface, very different from its cratered neighbors Ganymede and Calisto. *Cassini*, a probe studying Saturn and its moons, captured incredible views of water erupting from fissures, or cracks, near Enceladus's south pole.

These observations all point to large, sub-surface oceans locked beneath these moons' icy crusts. Even though their surfaces are frozen, the interiors of both are thought to be kept warm by tidal forces that stretch and compress their rocky cores, generating enough heat to keep the subsurface oceans from freezing.

If there is life in these distant subsurface oceans, it would likely never see sunlight. Any alien organisms need to get their energy another way.

We've seen this with certain extremophiles on Earth, such as the organisms living near deep-ocean volcanic vents that don't need sunlight to survive. What kinds of life might evolve in a deep alien ocean without sunlight? A NASA mission under development to visit Europa is planning to explore it from orbit. NASA might even send a lander to the surface.

ICY JETS

NASA's *Cassini* orbiter has spotted jets of water erupting into space from the surface of Enceladus. What might that mean for the search for life? Watch this video to learn more.

🔍 Enceladus is an Active World

Enceladus

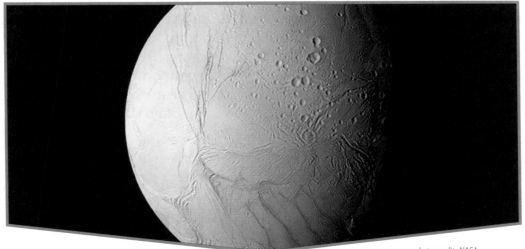

photo credit: NASA

BEYOND THE SOLAR SYSTEM: EXOPLANETS

HUNTING FOR ALIEN WORLDS

The number of exoplanets discovered is always increasing. Check out this website to follow the latest on the search for alien worlds!

🔍 NASA exoplanet exploration

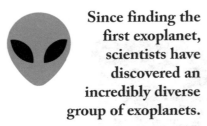

Since finding the first exoplanet, scientists have discovered an incredibly diverse group of exoplanets.

Science fiction stories are full of worlds beyond our solar system. From the moon Pandora in the film *Avatar* to Vulcan in the *Star Trek* television series, the Milky Way of science fiction has been teeming with life for more than 100 years. But astronomers didn't find evidence that extrasolar planets, or exoplanets, even existed until the 1990s!

Even with giant telescopes on Earth and the Hubble Telescope in space, seeing a planet around a distant star is very hard to do. The stars are so bright that it's impossible to see a small exoplanet orbiting it. It's like trying to see a lit match next to a spotlight. So, instead of looking directly for planets, astronomers look at the stars they orbit.

To say that planets orbit stars isn't entirely true. Both stars and planets exert a gravitational pull on one another. As a result, the two actually orbit a place where the forces balance, called the barycenter. The barycenter is always closer to the more massive object.

Because most planets are very small compared to their suns, the barycenter is often inside the star itself, which is why it looks like the planet orbits the star. But the larger the planet, the stronger its pull is on the star and the closer the barycenter is to the planet. As a star swings around this common center, it seems to wobble slightly. Astronomers can observe and measure this wobble. That's how they find exoplanets.

As the star wobbles, there can be a slight change in the star's spectrum. When the star moves toward an observer, the spectrum appears slightly more blue, and when it moves away the spectrum appears slightly more red.

WHAT?! YOU'RE SAYING THAT THE EARTH ISN'T ORBITING THE SUN?

WELL, NOT EXACTLY. LET ME SHOW YOU ON MY LAPTOP

STARS AND THEIR PLANETS EXERT GRAVITATIONAL PULL ON EACH OTHER.

BARYCENTER

THEY ACTUALLY ORBIT THE POINT WHERE THE FORCES BALANCE.

THAT POINT'S CALLED THE BARYCENTER.

WHO'S THIS BARRY AND WHY DOES HE GET HIS OWN CENTER?

[If these changes in the star's light repeat themselves, there might be a planet tugging on the star!]

This method has its drawbacks. It's a good way to find large, gas planets, such as Jupiter, because their star's wobble is more pronounced and easier to see. Finding smaller planets this way can be much harder. The wobble they produce is small, and if their orbits are similar to Earth's, it can take years to see a pattern. Fortunately, there's another way.

ALIEN ECLIPSES

Have you ever seen an eclipse? When the moon passes between the sun and your position on Earth, it can block out part or even all of the sun's light, casting a shadow. On Earth, we see this as a solar eclipse.

The moon isn't the only thing that can block the sun's light. When Mercury or Venus passes between the sun and the Earth, it's called a transit. Both planets are so far away that they can't completely block out the sun from our earthly perspective. Instead, with the right equipment, we can see their small disks crossing the sun.

The same thing happens with exoplanets orbiting distant stars. When an exoplanet passes between us and its host star, the transit causes the star's light to dim slightly. The small but measurable dip in light can alert astronomers to the presence of an exoplanet.

There are other things that can dim a star's light, such as sunspots or large clouds of dust and gas. To tell the difference between a transiting planet and some other phenomena, astronomers look for a regular dip in light. Seeing just one dip isn't enough. The frequency of dips tells astronomers the length of the exoplanet's year.

[
Because some exoplanets might take more than one Earth year to orbit their sun, it can take a long time to be certain that an exoplanet has been found.
]

To see these small dips in light from a distant star, astronomers need very sensitive telescopes that are free of any interference from our own atmosphere. NASA launched the Kepler space telescope in 2009 to get a good look at exoplanet transits. From its position orbiting the sun, the telescope stares at one patch of sky, watching 100,000 stars at once for a telltale dip in a star's light caused by an extrasolar transit.

How do these exoplanets compare to our own planet? What makes a world habitable and what should we be looking for?

SCI-FI FACT

So far, the Kepler space telescope has confirmed the existence of more than 1,000 exoplanets, and there is more data for astronomers to analyze.

THE GOLDILOCKS ZONE

Earth sits in a special place in the solar system. If it were closer to the sun, it might have turned out like Venus, destroyed by a runaway greenhouse effect and left with surface temperatures hot enough to melt lead. Farther from the sun, Earth might have turned out like Mars, cold and dry, with the bulk of its water locked away in ice.

Instead, we have a planet with rivers, lakes, and oceans, as well as continents with mountains, plains, and valleys. And all of it is covered with life. We live on a planet that sits inside our star's Goldilocks Zone, or habitable zone. It's the area that is just the right distance from the sun for liquid water to exist on the surface.

Every star has a habitable zone, which depends on the star's luminosity. This is the amount of energy a star puts out. Stars with a higher luminosity will have habitable zones farther away than stars with a lower luminosity.

Earth is a terrestrial, or rocky, planet with a solid surface. Many of the exoplanets discovered so far are gas giants, similar to Jupiter and Saturn. When it comes to looking for exoplanets that could harbor life, astronomers look for rocky worlds a little larger or smaller than Earth that sit within the habitable zone of their stars. So far, scientists have found a few.

Unfortunately, we can't travel to investigate distant exoplanets ourselves just yet, but we can still glean a lot of information about these worlds from a distance. Even detecting these exoplanets tells us a lot about them, such as their mass, diameter, density, and length of year. But it doesn't tell us if they're capable of supporting life. When considering how to look for life on an exoplanet, we have to start with what we know, which is life on Earth.

A PLANET AROUND PROXIMA

An Earth-sized planet has been discovered orbiting our nearest stellar neighbor, Proxima Centauri. The planet Proxima b orbits within the dwarf star's Goldilocks Zone and has a year that is only 11 days long! Check out this link to learn more about the newest planet in our neighborhood!

🔍 ESO discovers Earth-size planet

THE SIGNATURE OF LIFE

To find evidence of life on exoplanets, astronomers and astrobiologists look for biosignatures, or evidence that life might live in the atmosphere. For example, on Earth, the oxygen we breathe is made mostly by plants, so finding traces of oxygen in the atmosphere of a rocky exoplanet might indicate that some form of life is present. However, oxygen can come from natural geologic processes that have nothing to do with life.

The water cycle on Earth ensures that water can be detected in our atmosphere. Although we're pretty sure life means water, water doesn't necessarily mean life.

Finding a signal of pollution might be more important. Greenhouse gases are produced on Earth by manufacturing and energy production. Gases such as carbon monoxide and ozone could be proof that an intelligent civilization is on the planet and going through an industrial revolution. To find evidence of life on other planets, we need an even bigger telescope.

The James Webb Space Telescope, when launched in 2018, will be the largest and most powerful telescope ever used in space. One of its missions will be to examine the atmospheres of exoplanets and look for evidence of gases such as oxygen and methane. However, its spectrometer isn't sensitive enough to detect them in atmospheres as thin as Earth's.

In order to study planets with Earth-like atmospheres, an even larger telescope than the James Webb Space Telescope will be needed in the future.

LISTENING FOR ALIENS

Looking for evidence of life on exoplanets is only one way to look for alien life. In addition to observing the atmospheres of exoplanets, we can also listen for alien signals.

In the 1997 movie *Contact*, radio astronomer Elli Arroway detects a mysterious radio signal. She and her team quickly realize that the signal is something special. It's repeating a list of prime numbers, something natural and manmade radio sources wouldn't do. After trying and failing to explain it in any other way, they decide it might be an alien civilization sending a message.

Humans have been broadcasting radio and television signals into space for nearly 100 years. Since all electromagnetic radiation travels through space at the speed of light, any advanced civilization within 100 light years might be able to receive these signals if they're listening. It's reasonable to think that an advanced alien civilization might be broadcasting, too. How do we listen for them?

SEARCHING SPACE

In 1977, a scientist in Ohio named Jerry R. Ehman, working as a volunteer at the Big Ear radio telescope, found something interesting on a printout of radio signals. The signal was loud, so strong that he wrote "Wow!" on the print out.

photo credit: Big Ear Radio Observatory and North American AstroPhysical Observatory

What do you think will happen if we contact or even meet an intelligent civilization?

Other radio telescopes around the world turned their dishes to the signal's location in the sky, hoping it might be a signal from another world. But they turned up nothing.

Although the "Wow!" signal was never seen again, its discovery helped build a scientific program to look for evidence of alien broadcasts. The Search for Extraterrestrial Intelligence (SETI) is a program by scientists to look for signs of intelligent life in the universe. For nearly 50 years, SETI has combed through data from radio telescopes around the world, looking for signals that can't be explained by natural or man-made sources. So far, there have been no signals that haven't been explained, but the search continues.

The first evidence of intelligent life in the universe would be an incredible event. It would likely affect our views on science, religion, and philosophy, just to start. Science fiction stories tackle this idea of first contact in many different ways. Some, such as the movie *Independence Day*, feature aliens as monsters, determined to take over the planet with a culture and biology very different from our own. Others films, such as *E.T.: The Extraterrestrial*, portray loveable and kind aliens, showing us to be the monsters.

[Even today, extraterrestrials of science fiction bear a lot of similarities to humans, but any aliens out there might look and act very differently.]

Life on Earth came from a unique set of circumstances starting about 4.5 billion years ago. From the first single-celled organisms to plants and animals, evolution has allowed life to exist in almost every earthly environment imaginable.

But what might life look like on a world covered in water or one with low gravity? Organisms on other planets are likely to face very different obstacles, challenges, and environments as they evolve. There's no way of knowing what they might look like or if they'll be intelligent.

What are the chances of even finding anyone in a place the size of the Milky Way?

IS ANYONE OUT THERE?

Is it possible we're the only intelligent creatures in the universe? Modern humans have been around for only 200,000 years, surviving natural and manmade disasters along the way. We live on Earth, the only planet in our solar system that can sustain life. Earth orbits the sun, a relatively calm and well-behaved star, at a distance that is just the right temperature to keep us alive.

In the last century, we've developed radio and television. For nearly 100 years our music and television shows have been traveling into space in every direction, signaling our existence to anything that might be listening.

Astronomers estimate there might be as many as a septillion stars in the universe. It's reasonable to think that some of these stars might have planets, and that some of these planets might develop intelligent life with the technology to signal us.

So just how many of these intelligent, communicating civilizations might there be? We could be the only intelligent civilization. Other guesses put the number at 10 million advanced civilizations in the galaxy. As we continue to explore, science should help us answer the question once and for all.

AN ADVOCATE FOR EARTH AND SPACE

Carl Sagan (1934–1996) was a celebrated astronomer, author, and science communicator. He hosted the PBS television series *Cosmos*, and wrote the novel *Contact*, which was later made into a movie. He is considered to be one of the all-time greatest popularizers of science. Listen to an interview with Sagan in which he talks about aliens and the influence of science fiction on real science.

 Carl Sagan alien civilizations

WILL THEY COME IN PEACE?

Science fiction really has only two kinds of aliens—those that hate humans and those that don't. There are stories of wars with aliens and plots to steal Earth from us. There are also tales of kindly extraterrestrials that help and guide humanity, or at least tolerate us.

Again, we can only look at what we know, and that's ourselves. Humans have flaws. We have crime, war, and manmade climate change, for example. But we're also capable of curiosity and kindness and hope.

In the 1970s, the *Voyager* probes' grand tour of the outer planets took them on a one-way journey out of the solar system on their way to interstellar space. A team led by astronomer and writer Carl Sagan created two Golden Records that were installed on both *Voyagers 1* and *2*. The disks contained recorded sounds and images of life on Earth from around the world. On their surface, the discs showed an image of a man and woman, as well as a map to find Earth based on nearby pulsars.

Even though the chances of the disk being discovered by an intelligent civilization are extremely small (it will be 40,000 years before either probe comes close to another star), it was viewed as a celebration of mankind. Sagan said:

"The spacecraft will be encountered and the record played only if there are advanced spacefaring civilizations in interstellar space. But the launching of this bottle into the cosmic ocean says something very hopeful about life on this planet."

We can hope only that any intelligent life we might meet one day is no better or worse than we are.

KEY QUESTIONS

- What are some of the challenges of finding life on other planets?
- Could there be life on other planets that isn't carbon based and doesn't need water to survive?
- What do you think it would be like to be contacted by aliens from another planet? How would you react?

"A MESSAGE IN A BOTTLE CAST INTO THE COSMIC SEA" —CARL SAGAN

In 1977, *Voyager 1* and *Voyager 2* were launched to study the outer solar system. They provided us with the first close-up pictures of Jupiter, Saturn, Uranus, and Neptune, and continue to provide valuable information about the solar system on their way to interstellar space. Both *Voyagers* are also carrying a message from Earth in the form of a Golden Record. Although the chances are very, very small that any civilization will come across these probes, if they do, they'll be able to learn about the civilization that sent them on their journey.

- **Imagine you have the opportunity to compose a message to an alien civilization.** What would you put in the message? Would you tell them about your life? Would you tell them about Earth, history, and culture? What pictures or sounds might you include?

- **Create a message.** What would you want a distant civilization to know about you and your life? What would you share about the world you live in? Would you discuss current events, history, or art? What would you want to know about them?

- **Put it together.** You can include pictures, video, writings, drawings, and sound in your message. Speak with family, friends, or classmates—what would they include in a message to the stars?

To investigate further, choose an exoplanet to send your message to. Why did you choose that particular exoplanet? How long will it take your message to arrive? How long would it be before you could expect a reply?

THE DRAKE EQUATION: IS ANYONE OUT THERE?

In the 1960s, astronomer Frank Drake was thinking about how many intelligent civilizations might exist in the Milky Way galaxy. He developed the Drake Equation, which is a useful tool to try to estimate the number.

$$N = R^* \cdot f_p \cdot n_e \cdot f_l \cdot f_i \cdot f_c \cdot L$$

- **It helps to first look at the parts separately:**

  - N = Is there anyone out there? This is the number of estimated civilizations in the galaxy, or the number the Drake Equation gives us.

  - R^* = The number of stars born in our galaxy each year.

  - f_p = The fraction of those stars that form planets.

  - n_e = The number of those planets that have the right conditions for life (as we know it).

  - f_l = The fraction of those planets that actually develop life.

  - f_i = The fraction of planets with life that becomes intelligent.

  - f_c = The fraction of intelligent civilizations that are detectable.

  - L = The length of time those civilizations broadcast signals we can detect.

- **Because many of the variables are hard to know, the answer can be very different, depending on who you ask!** What's your estimate?

- **Here are some values that are thought to be well known.**

  - $R^* = 7$ The rate of star formation in our galaxy is thought to be about seven per year.

  - $f_p = 1$ It's now thought that most stars form planets. To keep it simple, make $fp = 1$, meaning 100 percent of stars form planets.

  - For the rest of the values, think about what each one means and make your own guesses.

- **Fill in your values.** Once you've chosen your numbers, copy the chart and fill in your values. Now you should be able to estimate how many intelligent civilizations there might be in the galaxy! Why did you choose the values you used?

  - Try the equation with different variables. What happens if every planet with life develops intelligent life ($fi = 1$), for example?

  - Can any of the variables be 0? What happens if they are?

  - How does changing other values of the equation affect N? Remember, this is the number of civilizations in the galaxy.

  - What is your lowest estimate? What is your highest estimate?

- **Compare your results with those of someone else—a classmate, a friend, or a family member.**

  - Are your results the same or different? Why?

  - What conclusions can you draw? How common is intelligent life in the galaxy?

> To investigate further, compare your estimates to those of a friend or classmate. Are they similar or different? What did they choose for their variables and why?

CITIZEN SCIENCE: REAL SCIENCE YOU CAN DO AT HOME

Would you like to help look for the next exoplanet or listen for signals from an alien civilization? You can contribute to real research and help scientists around the world analyze data on your own, from your own home. Scientists often collect so much data that it can take years or even decades to analyze all of it. Citizen science helps move research forward by giving people the chance to help sort through and analyze data much more quickly than scientists could do on their own.

- **Choose a program.** Select a citizen science program. Why did you choose that particular program? What kind of data are you working with? What are you helping research?

  - At Zooniverse.org, you can be a planet hunter! In their planet hunter project, you learn to use real data from the Kepler space telescope and look for the tell-tale patterns of planets transiting their stars. You can also help study the weather on Mars, look for asteroids, and classify galaxies! There are more than 44 different activities to choose from at this site, all involving real science.

    🔍 zooniverse

  - SETI@Home uses your computer to analyze radio signals from space, looking for signs of intelligent life. It can run as a screensaver or in the background when your computer isn't being used. Although it isn't an interactive program such as Zooniverse, you can see the area of sky your computer is analyzing and the result from each piece of data your computer studies.

    🔍 SETI@Home

> To investigate further, challenge friends or family to participate in a citizen science program. Why did they choose their particular programs, and what kind of research are they doing? See who can complete the most datasets!

Chapter 5

Faster-Than-Light Travel

Why is it useful to
travel faster than
the speed of light?

Panel 1: OUR NEAREST STELLAR NEIGHBOR IS PROXIMA CENTAURI. AT THE SPEED OF LIGHT IT WOULD TAKE FOUR YEARS TO GET THERE!

Panel 2: IF I COULD FLY AT THE SPEED OF LIGHT THAT'S NOT WHERE I'D GO.

Panel 3: WHERE WOULD YOU GO? SIRIUS? BARNARD'S STAR? NO. I'D GO TO ITALY FOR SOME FRESH PIZZA! I'M STARVING!

If we could travel faster than the speed of light, we could explore far more distant parts of the galaxy.

In science fiction, traveling across the galaxy is easy. Spaceships in *Star Trek* use warp drive, while ships in *Star Wars* use hyper drives to cross unimaginable distances in as little time as we take to leave town on a weekend road trip. Even though our solar system might seem huge from our perspective, compared to the galaxy and the universe, it's tiny. If it takes months or years for our space probes to reach Mars and Jupiter, will we ever be able to cross the vast distances between stars the way they do in books and movies?

HOW BIG IS SPACE?

Space is really big. Our nearest celestial neighbor, the moon, is more than 240,000 miles away. If you drove that distance at a speed of 100 miles per hour, it would take you more than three months to reach your destination.

Even the fastest rocket-propelled spacecraft ever built took a long time to reach its target. Launched in 2006 and traveling about 36,000 miles per hour, *New Horizons* took nine years to travel the 3 billion miles to Pluto. Stars are even farther away. The nearest star that isn't our sun is more than 5,000 times as far as Pluto. It would take *New Horizons* about 45,000 years to get there!

THE SPEED OF LIGHT

No matter how powerful a rocket or how futuristic a technology, nothing can travel through space faster than light. Light is the fastest thing in the universe. It takes photons of light only 8.5 minutes to travel the 92,000,000 miles from the sun to the Earth. That's about 186,282 miles per second, or 670,616,629 miles per hour. Knowing how incredibly fast light moves makes it possible to understand how far away the stars are. Our nearest stellar neighbor, Proxima Centauri, is 24,900,000,000,000 miles away. It takes the light from Alpha Centauri more than four years to reach us on Earth!

Once astronomers figured out how far away stars really are, they realized they needed a better way to describe those distances. The numbers are simply too big when using miles or kilometers! Their solution was the light year, the distance light travels in one year, or 5,878,499,810,000 miles. When we talk about Alpha Centauri, we don't say it's 24,900,000,000,000 miles away—we say it's a little more than four light years from Earth.

This term also tells us something about the light we're seeing. If the star we observe is 15 light years away, the light left that star 15 years ago and is only now reaching our eyes. We don't see the stars as they are now, we see them as they were then.

WHERE IS THE NEAREST STAR?

Proxima Centauri is actually part of a system of three stars. Alpha Centauri A is slightly larger than our sun, while Alpha Centauri B is slightly smaller. Proxima Centauri is a type of star called a red dwarf. The Alpha Centauri system is a popular destination in science fiction and is visible from the Southern Hemisphere in the constellation Centaurus. Because they are so far away, the A and B appear to be one star to the naked eye!

ROCKET SCIENCE

Knowing the distance to a star tells us how long it would take to travel there—if we could move at the speed of light. But that's not easy. How fast can our current forms of propulsion take us?

Today's chemical rockets haven't changed much since the early rockets of Robert Goddard and Werner von Braun. Chemical rockets work by burning fuel and oxidizer to produce thrust. Liquid fuel rocket engines keep their fuel and oxidizer in separate tanks until it's time to launch. Then they are combined and the mixture is ignited. Solid fuel rockets have their oxidizer and fuel combined in a solid mass that starts producing thrust as soon as it's ignited.

Regardless of the kind of rocket, once the fuel and oxidizer ignite, hot gas is expelled from the engine with tremendous force. We know from Sir Isaac Newton's third law of motion that the reactive force propels the spaceship in the opposite direction of the escaping gas, creating thrust.

Liquid engines are extremely complicated, but they can be throttled, shut off, and even restarted. Solid engines are simple, and once they're lit they can't be turned off.

Sir Isaac Newton's third law of motion states that for every action, there is an equal and opposite reaction.

Proxima Centauri, our closest stellar neighbor

photo credit: ESA/Hubble & NASA

Both solid and liquid fuel rockets have taken people and payloads into space for more than 50 years. They work well for traveling the relatively short distance to low Earth orbit or even the moon. But if you want to go faster and farther, especially with passengers, chemical rockets aren't a great choice. They're very inefficient. Only about 35 percent of their energy is actually turned into thrust. Chemical rockets have to carry all the fuel they need with them, in addition to the spacecraft and everything human passengers might need on a journey.

[
It takes a lot of energy to lift all this mass off Earth, and the heavier the rocket, the more fuel it needs. More fuel means even more weight.
]

The most powerful rocket ever created was *Saturn V*, which took *Apollo* astronauts to the moon. It weighed more than 6 million pounds at launch and was only able to get 97,000 pounds to the moon at a top speed of nearly 25,000 miles per hour. Although it's 50 times faster than a passenger jet, it can't go even 1/10,000 of the speed of light. What can we use other than chemical fuel to push us closer to the speed of light?

DAWN—THE REAL TIE FIGHTER

The fictional TIE fighter from *Star Wars* gets its name from its "twin ion engines," which make it a speedy and maneuverable craft capable of engaging the fighters of the Rebel Alliance. NASA's *DAWN* spacecraft was the first real spacecraft to use an ion engine rather than chemical propulsion on its mission to the asteroid Vesta and the dwarf planet Ceres. But *DAWN* doesn't look or move much like a TIE fighter.

ROCKET MEN

Robert Goddard and Werner von Braun played major roles in the development of rocketry. Robert Goddard designed and launched the first liquid-fueled rocket in 1926, while Von Braun helped design *Saturn V*, the most powerful rocket every built. You can see Goddard performing test flights of his rockets here.

PS

Goddard 1926 video

Light can circle Earth more than seven times in one second, more than a million times faster than a passenger plane.

Ion engines, also called electric propulsion, generate thrust by using a very light gas, such as xenon, and a small amount of electricity. When an atom of xenon gains or loses an electron, it becomes positively or negatively charged—this is an ion. This ionized gas is propelled out of the rocket engine at a very high speed, but because the gas is so light it produces only a small amount of thrust. This means ion engines aren't powerful enough to lift anything off the earth, but they work very well in deep space.

Ion engines have one very important advantage over chemical rockets—they can operate for many years using very little fuel, slowly but surely building up a lot of speed. This means that they're extremely efficient. Nearly 90 percent of the energy they generate moves the spacecraft forward.

Because it's such a small push, the technology as it is today is only good for accelerating payloads much smaller than a spacecraft with a crew on board. Scientists are working at finding ways to improve ion drives. They estimate that new versions of these futuristic thrusters could propel a spacecraft up to 200,000 miles per hour.

A drawing of *DAWN* (right) compared to a TIE fighter

photo credit: NASA/JPL

This is still only 0.02 percent the speed of light. Even if an ion engine accelerated continuously for many years, it still wouldn't come close to the speed of light. Ion engines are not yet powerful enough to travel between stars in a reasonable amount of time.

THE NUCLEAR OPTION

In the 1950s and 1960s, the Atomic Age saw the development of nuclear-powered submarines, nuclear power plants, and many different kinds of nuclear weapons. Even today, harnessing the power of the atom provides incredible amounts of energy from very small amounts of nuclear fuel.

Rocket scientists determined that a nuclear rocket engine could be much more powerful and twice as efficient as a chemical rocket, getting a crew to Mars in a matter of weeks instead of months. One concept, called Project Orion, even proposed detonating small nuclear bombs behind a spaceship to accelerate it to speeds up to 3 percent the speed of light.

There are some drawbacks to using nuclear engines. Rockets don't always launch perfectly, meaning there's always a chance the engine could explode and destroy the spacecraft in the process. If a nuclear-powered rocket exploded during launch, it could spread deadly radiation across a wide area. These concerns and a lack of funding caused the program to be canceled in the 1970s.

Recently, scientists resumed research on nuclear rockets. NASA is testing a nuclear thermal engine that could propel spacecraft between the planets in our solar system in very short periods of time. However, even a nuclear rocket won't be powerful enough for a crew to reach another star during a lifetime.

EINSTEIN AND RELATIVITY

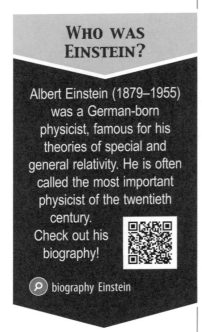

Even if we use these future propulsion technologies, Albert Einstein revealed that the nature of light itself provides a speed limit that is impossible to overcome. In 1905, Einstein published his theory of special relativity. With it, he showed that the speed of light is the fastest anything can travel through space, and this speed is always the same no matter where you are in the universe. The speed of light is a constant and everything else depends on your point of view, even time and space.

Have you ever been sitting in a car at a stoplight and felt as though you were moving backward? And then you realize—it's the car next to you that's moving forward! Your perception of the other car gives you a sense of motion, and you can't tell who's actually moving until you notice that you're still stopped at the light.

On Earth, we need a fixed reference point, such as the road or a stoplight, to tell who is moving and who isn't. But what would happen if you had no other reference points, if you could only see yourself and the other car?

Imagine two lonely astronauts drifting past each other in deep space, far from any stars or planets. With nothing nearby to compare their motion to, they have no way of deciding who is moving and who isn't. This is an example of how motion is relative and how it affects the way we measure an object's speed.

When we travel on Earth, we measure our speed relative to the ground beneath us. But Earth itself is moving. It's turning on its axis to give us a 24-hour day. Earth is also orbiting the sun, and the sun is hurtling around the center of the Milky Way galaxy at about a million miles per hour.

> In fact, everything in the universe is moving, meaning that you can calculate your speed only by comparing it to something else.

Einstein thought of this, though, and realized that not only are speed and motion relative, time can be relative, too. The sound of thunder from a storm overhead will reach your ears before it reaches your friend listening on the other side of town. Although you both agree that you heard thunder, you'll disagree on when you heard it.

Imagine riding a skateboard toward your best friend, who is standing still. Once you reach a speed of 20 miles per hour, you throw a baseball to her at 40 miles per hour. How fast will she measure the speed of your pitch when it hits her glove? It's your speed on the skateboard plus the speed of the ball:

20 mph + 40 mph = 60 mph

Relative to you, the ball is traveling at 40 miles per hour, but relative to her, the ball is moving at 60 mph. What happens if, instead of tossing a baseball, you toss a beam of light?

Imagine riding your skateboard toward your best friend as you shine a flashlight toward her. What do you think she'll measure the speed at? You might assume that she'd measure the speed of the beam as the speed of light plus the speed of your skateboard, but, strangely, this isn't how it works. If you were both to measure the speed of the light, you would get exactly the same result.

How is this possible? Einstein realized that the speed of light is absolute, that it never changes no matter how it's measured. For the speed of light to stay constant, some incredible things happen when you try to catch up with a photon of light.

The only thing in the universe that is not relative is the speed of light.

One of the first to measure the speed of light, Danish astronomer Olaus Roemer (1644–1710) used the movement of Jupiter and its moons to arrive at a speed of 132,973 miles per second—not too bad for the year 1676!

RACING LIGHT

If you left Earth in a ship traveling at 99 percent the speed of light, you wouldn't notice anything strange inside your spacecraft. But your best friend watching as you leave Earth would see some very strange things. First, she would notice that the length of your ship and everything in it had shrunk in the direction you were traveling, including you! Second, if she could measure your mass, she would see that the mass of you and your ship had increased. Finally, and maybe most incredibly, your friend would observe you moving around your ship in slow motion.

Meanwhile, as you look back at Earth, you would see some equally strange things. From your spacecraft, you would see your best friend and everyone on the planet moving extremely slow. If you and your best friend both measure the speed of light, you'd get exactly the same measurement. No matter how fast or slow you're moving, the speed of light doesn't change—but space and time can and do.

[
As something approaches the speed of light, time slows down, length contracts, and mass increases.
]

Because of this, the faster you go, the more energy it takes to increase your speed. In fact, reaching the speed of light is impossible, because to do so, your mass and the energy needed to move it would become infinite, your length would shrink to zero, and time for you would stop.

This is the cosmic speed limit—reaching it would require an infinite amount of energy. For this reason, most scientists believe that reaching light speed is impossible . . . but there might be another way.

If we can never travel faster than light though space, how can we explore the galaxy? Science fiction solves this problem by taking shortcuts through black holes, wormholes, and even bending space itself. Are any of these ideas supported by real science?

COSMIC SHORTCUTS

Have you ever taken a shortcut? You can make a long trip easier by finding a more direct route. In science fiction, short cuts through space are created by warp drives, wormholes, and black holes, all of which bend space in some way. By curving space, science fiction authors are able to avoid the cosmic speed limit and visit the stars.

In 1916, in his theory of general relativity, Einstein described how gravity can warp space. To imagine how this works, think of a tennis ball sitting on a mattress. If nothing disturbs the mattress, the ball won't move, but if you step onto the bed it will roll toward your feet. Your weight produces a force that warps, or curves, the surface of the bed in the same way Einstein describes gravity warping space.

The more massive an object is, the more it bends space and time. Even Earth's gravity produces a very small but measurable effect. GPS satellites, for example, use very precise clocks in order to give you a precise location on Earth. If they didn't take into account the effects of special and general relativity, their clocks would not match ours on the ground, and your navigation app might send you to the wrong address.

The most extreme place to see the effects of general relativity is a black hole. At the core of every star is a process called nuclear fusion. This process produces enough energy that it stops the star from collapsing in on itself under its massive gravitational pull. However, when a star runs out of its fuel, it can't fight against the pull of gravity and the star collapses.

[If a star is massive enough, at the end of its life it becomes a black hole.]

LIGO

Recently, astrophysicists made an exciting discovery about gravitational waves. These waves were predicted by Einstein but difficult to observe until the development of LIGO, a set of observatories sensitive enough to pick up gravitational waves made by two black holes colliding 1.4 billion light years away. Learn more about LIGO at this website.

about LIGO

For a star to become a black hole, it needs to be about 10 times more massive than our sun. Stars that are less massive can become neutron stars or white dwarfs. Our star will probably become a white dwarf—in about 5 billion years!

BLACK HOLES IN THE MOVIES

In the science fiction movie *Interstellar*, space travelers get an up-close look at a black hole. The filmmakers consulted with astrophysicists to create a very accurate picture of what a black hole might look like. Check out the link to see how scientists made this happen.

🔍 Historic Gravitational Waves

Because a black hole is so dense and its gravity is so strong, nothing, not even light, can escape it. In fact, gravity is so extreme near a black hole that space and time become bent and warped.

The math and physics of a black hole is so difficult to understand that many science fiction stories take advantage of these unknowns and use them as shortcuts across the galaxy. Some sci-fi stories involve spaceships falling into black holes, only to be spit out in another place and time. But entering a black hole is not a good idea. Although nobody knows exactly what happens inside a black hole, we do know that if light can't escape, a spacecraft certainly can't.

Black holes aren't the only strange objects discussed by both science fiction writers and scientists. Wormholes were first dreamed up in 1935, when Einstein and fellow physicist Nathan Rosen used general relativity to suggest that a kind of interstellar bridge could connect distant points in space and time. Imagine a single sheet of paper with two dots 6 inches apart.

The shortest distance between the dots would be 6 inches, a straight line from one to the other. But you could shorten that distance by bending the paper and bringing the points closer to one another. And if you folded the paper so the two dots lay on top of each other, you would remove the distance between them entirely.

This is how physicists picture wormholes—bending or curving space so two distant points are lined up, shrinking the distance between them to nothing. Mathematically, relativity says this is possible, but you'd need things such as negative energy and negative mass to keep wormholes open long enough for a ship to fly through.

So far, physicists have no idea what negative energy or negative mass would be. Physicists also don't have firm evidence that wormholes even exist, but that doesn't mean they don't.

For the moment, wormholes exist only in fictional universes. But what about warp drives? In *Star Trek*, the *Enterprise* is able to journey between stars in very little time using its warp engines. Strangely, the crew doesn't have to deal with the effects of relativity— they don't leave on a voyage and return to find that everyone on Earth has aged decades while they've only been gone a few days.

According to calculations, wormholes are unstable, so it's possible that they simply don't last long enough for us to find them—let alone travel through them.

[
In *Star Trek*, no matter how fast they travel, their clocks always match the clocks back on Earth. And in fact, they travel at speeds beyond the speed of light!
]

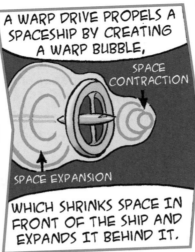

Interestingly enough, physics seems to say that this fiction might be turned into fact. Einstein showed us that nothing can travel through space faster than light. He also demonstrated that space can be warped, bent, and curved by gravity. Astrophysicist Miguel Alcubierre has proposed a ring-shaped warp drive that would cause space to shrink in front of a ship and expand behind it, creating a "warp bubble."

This bubble would carry a ship through space like a surfer rides a wave. The Alcubierre drive avoids the problems of relativity by keeping space flat inside the bubble and curving space around it. This could allow anything inside to travel many times faster than the speed of light without breaking the laws of physics.

Just like wormholes, there's a catch. Nobody knows how to create the amount of energy needed to shrink or expand space to make such a bubble. Physicists are looking for ways to do this, and if they can find it, we might just have a real warp drive in the future.

While traveling faster than the speed of light across the galaxy is unlikely to work, there are interesting ways that we might still explore our neighboring stars. Science fiction has imagined generational starships, huge vessels capable of supporting a group of explorers for decades or centuries as they travel from star to star. Scientists have proposed small robotic probes that could accelerate to terrific speeds for long periods of time through cutting-edge technology.

[
These could cross the distance to Alpha Centauri in many decades and send pictures and information on a four-year journey back to Earth.
]

While current understandings of physics keeps us from traveling faster than light through space, we've seen that there are possible ways to avoid the cosmic speed limit. We just need to figure out how to generate the incredible energies or produce the strange forms of matter these techniques require. After all, many people believed we'd never walk on the moon, and now we're planning a trip to Mars!

Fortunately, we have science fiction to help push our imaginations. Who knows what might happen in the future?

VOCAB LAB

Write down what you think each of the following words means. What root words can you find for help?

photon, **special relativity**, **warp drive**, **wormhole**, and **black hole**.

Compare your definitions with those of your friends or classmates. Did you all come up with the same meanings? Turn to the text and glossary if you need help.

KEY QUESTIONS

- **What are some of the obstacles to traveling at the speed of light?**
- **What are some ways scientists are working to solve these obstacles?**
- **Can you imagine other ways of traveling at or beyond the speed of light?**

MEASURING THE SPEED OF LIGHT

Einstein showed that nothing can travel faster than the speed of light, which is an incredible 186,282 miles per second or 299,792,463 meters per second. But you don't need to be Einstein to measure the cosmic speed limit, you just need a microwave and some chocolate! Sweet!

Microwave ovens use microwaves to heat food. Microwaves are a kind of electromagnetic radiation like light waves and X-rays. All electromagnetic radiation travels at the speed of light, and if we measure the speed of the microwaves, we've measured the speed of light!

- **Prepare your microwave.** If your microwave has a rotating plate inside, remove it and put a microwave safe plate upside-down on the rotator. You want the chocolate to stay put.

- **Prepare your chocolate.** Unwrap a bar of chocolate and place it at the center of the plate. It doesn't need to be covered. Don't eat it!

- **Nuke it.** Heat the chocolate until you see two or three spots begin to melt. This should take no more than 20 seconds. When finished, let the chocolate cool for 1 or 2 minutes.

- **Measure the chocolate.** Once it's cooled off, remove the plate and chocolate from the microwave. Using a ruler, measure the distance between the melted spots in centimeters, and convert it to meters by dividing by 100.

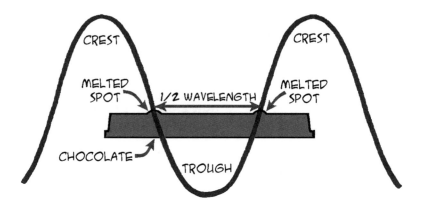

- **To calculate the speed of the microwaves we need to know their wavelength and frequency.** Light travels in waves, and the distance between the melted spots of chocolate is half of a wavelength. So we need to multiply your measurement by 2 to find out the wavelength.

- **Next, we need to know the frequency of the microwave, or how quickly the wave moves up and down per second.** Most microwaves work at a frequency of 2.45 gigahertz, which means the waves move up and down 2.45 billion times per second! Have someone check your microwave's manual or label to make sure this is the frequency of your microwave.

- **Calculate the speed of wave.** Finally, we can calculate the speed of the wave by using this formula:

    Speed of wave = wavelength x frequency

- **Your answer will be in meters per second.** How does it compare to the speed of light?

To investigate further, research other ways people have measured the speed of light. Are there other ways you could do it at home?

Ideas for Supplies ▼

- balloons
- straws

To investigate further, consider other types of rockets that you can build and launch at home. Some use water pressure to propel them forward, while others use small versions of solid fuel rockets! What kind would you like to try?

BALLOON ROCKETS

Rockets have been around for hundreds of years, but only recently have they started taking humans into space. Rockets generate a force called thrust by combining fuel and oxidizer and igniting them, which pushes the rocket through the air and into space. You can see how thrust can propel an object by using the air pressure inside a balloon!

- **Support the string.** Tie one end of the string to something that won't move, such as a doorknob or a heavy chair.

- **Mount the straw.** Slide the straw onto the string, and tie the other end of the string to another support. Make sure that the string is fairly tight, and doesn't sag too much.

- **Pressurize the balloon.** Blow up the balloon and pinch off the mouth to keep the air inside. Don't tie it!

- **Attach the balloon.** While keeping the mouth of the balloon closed, tape the balloon to the straw so that the mouth is horizontal to the ground.

- **Launch it!** Pull the balloon to one end of the string, and let go of the mouth.

  - What happens? What forces are acting?

  - Try measuring the time it takes for the balloon to cross the length of the string. How does the amount of air in the balloon affect the distance it travels and the speed of the balloon?

  - Try adding a payload by taping different objects to the balloon. How does weight affect the performance of the balloon?

Chapter 6 ▶
Time Travel

Is it possible to travel in time?

In science fiction stories, characters often travel back and forth in time to solve their problems, while sometimes creating new problems. In real life, no one has ever traveled in time—yet.

Have you ever wanted to travel back in time? Maybe you'd like to study harder for a test or have lunch with Abraham Lincoln or see how dinosaurs lived? What about traveling to the future to see how the world looks 10, 100, or even 1,000 years from now? Heroes in science fiction stories use time travel to learn about the past or future, fix mistakes, and change history, but it doesn't always work out well for them.

One classic tale of time travel is H.G. Wells's 1895 novel, *The Time Machine*. In the story, an inventor describes time as a fourth dimension and claims to be able to travel in time the same way he can travel through a town. His friends find this hard to believe, but the inventor proves them wrong. He returns a week later from the year 802,701 and delights his friends with stories of a terrifying future from which he was lucky to escape. Although *The Time Machine* was one of the first stories to describe traveling in time, it certainly wasn't the last.

Other science fiction stories explore traveling back in time and the unintended consequences this can have. Imagine traveling back to the Ford Theater on the night of Lincoln's assassination and preventing it from happening. If Lincoln survives, how would it change history? Time travel stories like these are filled with problems that will make your brain ache.

[
Never mind the complications of time travel—is traveling into the past or future even possible?
]

THE GRANDFATHER PARADOX AND OTHER PROBLEMS

Traveling back in time sounds amazing, but changing the past could affect the future in ways that could be hard to predict. Imagine your trip back in time accidentally keeps you from being born! This is known as the Grandfather Paradox, and this paradox creates some pretty big problems for anyone hoping to travel into the past.

The Grandfather Paradox involves a time traveler interrupting their own timeline, causing them to never exist and making it impossible for them to go back in time in the first place. That's the paradox.

In the classic 1980s movie *Back to the Future*, teenager Marty McFly travels in time to the 1950s, where he accidentally keeps his parents from falling in love. As a result, his own timeline is changed and he is never born. And if he is never born, how could he travel back in time in the first place? A paradox like this seems to violate common sense, and it isn't the only problem with traveling to the past.

BACK TO THE FUTURE

Check out Marty McFly's return to 1985 in a time-traveling DeLorean sports car here!

🔍 Back to the Future DeLorean

Causality is the relationship between cause and effect—it's how we experience time. The order in which things happen in our universe is very important. For example, a broken window doesn't unexpectedly put itself back together again, and the ball that broke the window doesn't suddenly return to the hand that threw it. For us, time flows only in one direction. We never experience events in reverse, but it's a common topic in science fiction.

Many theorists have said that paradoxes and causal loops are proof that time travel into the past can't happen. They believe that the universe simply doesn't allow it.

Stephen Hawking's "chronology protection conjecture" states that in order to keep anyone from changing history, the laws of the universe will stop any attempt to travel to the past. If there's no time machine, paradoxes and contradictions won't exist, keeping time flowing in the right direction. But some theoreticians say otherwise, arguing that paradoxes and casual loops can be avoided thanks to quantum mechanics.

QUANTUM MECHANICS

Isaac Newton's laws of motion are the foundation of the physics we experience in our everyday lives. These laws of nature allow us to calculate the force needed to hit a home run, the path of a ball as it flies out of the park, and the speed at which it crashes through someone's window—all before it leaves the pitcher's hand.

While Newton's laws govern the world around us, things get very fuzzy when we try to use the same laws to describe the properties of subatomic particles such as electrons.

Electrons don't behave as bats and baseballs do, so we need a different set of laws to explain their properties. This set of laws is called quantum mechanics.

In the early 1900s, physicists were confused by the strange properties of light. In some experiments it behaved like a wave, spreading through space like ripples on the surface of a pond. In other experiments, it acted like particles that could be counted and measured individually. Unable to explain these strange characteristics, Albert Einstein realized that light, which is electromagnetic energy, came in distinct amounts, which he called quanta.

[This discovery allowed physicists to describe light as having the properties of both a wave and a particle, called a photon. This was the basis for quantum mechanics.]

In the 1920s, physicists began working out the details of quantum mechanics. Even physicists today admit that a lot of it sounds like science fiction.

According to quantum mechanics, the more you know about the speed of an electron, for example, the less you know about its location, and the more you know about its location, the less you know about its speed. In fact, for subatomic particles, you can never really know exactly where something is. You can only calculate the probability, or how likely it is to be somewhere at a certain time. This is called the uncertainty principle.

Imagine if this happened in baseball. If you tried to measure the speed of a pitch, you couldn't know where the ball will be when you need to hit it. If you know where the ball is, you couldn't know its speed.

THE REALM OF THE VERY SMALL

The three main subatomic particles are protons, which have positive charge, neutrons, which have a neutral charge, and electrons, which have negative charge. Together, they form atoms, which make up the matter we deal with every day. Everything is made of matter—even you!

The ball could be anywhere! How hard would it be to hit the ball? At best, you could only guess at where it might be at any time, and you wouldn't know what happened until you checked with the umpire.

Einstein himself wasn't comfortable with this idea at first, famously saying, "God doesn't play dice." But it's exactly this notion of many possible outcomes that science fiction writers and even some scientists think can help us avoid the paradoxes and contradictions of traveling back in time.

PARALLEL UNIVERSES

Quantum mechanics is all about probability. Only when a particle is measured do we know for sure which path it took. Until then, anything is possible. According to the many worlds version of quantum mechanics, anything that can happen to a particle does happen, but we only measure one outcome, or result. All the other possibilities occur, too, but in new and different universes! For example, if an umpire records the pitch as a strike in your universe, it's a ball in another universe.

Parallel universes give fictional time travelers a way out of paradoxes, contradictions, and loops by creating a new universe anytime the past is changed. Consider the Grandfather Paradox. If you accidentally keep your grandparents from meeting, that's okay. A new universe will be created in which you were never born, while the universe you come from still exists, and so do you. Paradoxes would no longer be an issue, giving time travelers the freedom to affect the past as much as they want.

The concept of parallel universes is only an idea—there is no actual evidence that other universes exist. It's a controversial idea. Many scientists argue both for and against it, and it's up to physicists to find proof.

The idea that something is unknown until it's measured is difficult to understand because there are so many possibilities that could happen. It's difficult for even the greatest physicists to make sense of how quantum physics works.

Quantum mechanics once seemed too strange to be true, but was then proved through the scientific process. The same could happen with parallel universes, if an experiment can be designed to prove or disprove their existence.

Even if time travel to the past is possible, and even if you could avoid paradoxes and causal loops through parallel universes, there's still the issue of actually going back in time. How could you do it?

Science fiction has no shortage of ideas on how to travel backward in time. Faster-than-light travel, black holes, and even sports cars have brought adventures from the present into the past. Could any of them actually work?

A number of sci-fi plots involve spaceships traveling faster than the speed of light, causing time to run backward and giving them access to the past. But as you get closer and closer to the speed of light, the laws of the universe make it impossible to actually reach such a speed by eventually needing more energy than exists in the entire universe. Although mathematically possible, so far there is no known way to break this speed limit.

Theoretical physicists have found other mathematical ways of traveling backward in time, but they require breaking other laws of physics by using exotic matter and energy, none of which are known to exist. Do you have any ideas on how to travel back to the past? What about traveling to the future?

EINSTEIN AND TIME TRAVEL TO THE FUTURE

Because 17,000 miles per hour is not very close to the speed of light, the amount of time travel that Scott Kelly experienced is small, but measurable.

Einstein's theories let us understand a lot more about space and time than we can experience in our daily lives. This includes time travel into the future. In chapter five, we learned that strange things happen to you as you approach the speed of light. Most importantly, we know that the faster you move relative to Earth, the slower the clock on board your very fast spacecraft moves compared to your friends' clocks back home.

Traveling at 50 percent of light speed, every 24 hours in your spaceship would be 27.7 hours on Earth. At 87 percent the speed of light, for every one day you travel, two days will go by on Earth. And at 99.99 percent the speed of light, just one day of traveling to you would be 71 days back on Earth.

This is real time travel. The math has been proven many times. Astronaut Scott Kelly spent a year orbiting the Earth at 17,000 miles per hour aboard the International Space Station. He came home a little less than $\frac{1}{100}$ of a second younger than his Earth-bound twin brother.

To see the future, all you need to do is leave Earth and return. Depending on how fast you travel and how long you are gone, time on Earth will move ahead at a much faster rate than time aboard your spaceship. Want to see what Earth will be like 10 years from now?

Moving at 99.99 percent of the speed of light relative to Earth, you'd need to travel for just 51 days—25.5 days out and 25.5 days back. How about 1,000 years? You'd need to take about a 14-year round trip.

While traveling to the future is possible, there's a catch—it's a one-way trip. Remember, there's still no way of going back in time that doesn't break the laws of physics. If you traveled to the future, you would never be able to tell your friend on Earth about it unless they went with you. Not to mention, the technology needed to travel anywhere near the speed of light doesn't exist yet.

LOOK UP!

There is, however, one way to travel back in time that breaks no laws, creates no paradoxes, and doesn't involve causal loops. All you need to do is look up.

Even though light is the fastest thing in the universe, it still takes time to travel the incredible distances between stars. Polaris, the north star, is nearly 434 light years away in the constellation Ursa Major. A light year is a measure of distance, but it also describes how long it takes light to cover a certain distance. Whenever you look at Polaris, you're seeing it as it was 434 years ago.

This is true of every star in the sky. If you know how far away it is in light years, you know how far back in time you're looking. And this works both ways. If an alien civilization on a planet orbiting Polaris was able to create a telescope powerful enough to see Earth, the aliens would see us as we were 434 years ago. They wouldn't see us as the technologically advanced, space-faring species we are today. And with a telescope that can see even farther into space, we can see further back in time. In fact, astronomers use telescopes to study the history of the universe, and learn more about the big bang. To learn about how the universe was created millions of years ago, we just need to build bigger and better telescopes.

SCI-FI FACT

While time travel to the future is possible, for now the best we can hope for is a few milliseconds if you're lucky enough to visit the International Space Station for a year or two.

KEY QUESTIONS

- **What is the connection between time and distance, according to quantum physics?**

- **How does the uncertainty principle prevent physicists from proving certain theories about quantum physics?**

TIME TRAVEL AGENCY

Suppose you owned your own time travel agency, taking people into the future by traveling near the speed of light. What would your business be like? What would your customers need to know before taking a trip? How far into the future would you take adventurers?

VOCAB LAB

Write down what you think each of the following words means. What root words can you find for help?

timeline, causal loop, causality, subatomic particle, quantum mechanics, quanta, and **uncertainty principle**.

Compare your definitions with those of your friends or classmates. Did you all come up with the same meanings? Turn to the text and glossary if you need help.

- **Design a brochure for your time travel business!** Devise a marketing strategy to convince people to travel in time.

- **Think of a name.** What would you call your time travel agency? You want it to be catchy!

- **Come up with a slogan.** What will you say to catch people's attention?

- **How far will you go?** What years in the future would your company visit?

- **What about the fine print?** Remember, time travel into the past isn't possible. It's important that your customers understand they'll only be traveling to the future! What effects of relativity do you think they should know about? What might cause them to have second thoughts?

> To investigate further, interview your friends and family. Would they take a one-way trip into the future? How far would they want to go? How about you?

CHANGING HISTORY

While we might not be able to travel into the past in real life, it's still possible in science fiction. If you could travel back in time and change history, where and when would you go? What would change?

- **Where and when would you go?** Decide on an event in history you'd like to change. Maybe you'd warn the captain of the *Titanic* about the icebergs in the North Atlantic. What about stopping a world leader from being assassinated, such as John F. Kennedy?

- **Research your topic.** How would history change as a result of your decision? How would the *Titanic*'s safe voyage across the Atlantic affect the future? What might President Kennedy have accomplished had he lived?

- **Create a timeline.** Using paper or a computer, construct an alternate timeline of history as a result of your changes to the past. What things would be different? Would anything stay the same?

- **Share your timeline.** What do your friends or family think of your changes to history? Can they think of any other outcomes, good or bad, that might happen?

To investigate further, ask yourself what would you change on your own timeline, and why? How would it affect your life, your family, and your friends? Create your own new timeline!

There are many movies and books that feature time travel. Do you have a favorite? What about your friends or family?

GLOSSARY

51 Pegasi b: the first exoplanet discovered by Doppler spectography.

airlock: in a spacecraft, two sets of doors that allow astronauts to move from a livable environment to space and back again without losing air.

amber: hardened tree sap that can preserve organisms that get trapped by it.

androids: robots that look and behave like people.

Apollo 8: the first crewed mission to fly around the moon in 1968.

arid: a climate that has very little or no rain.

artificial intelligence: also known as AI, the intelligence of a computer, program, or machine.

Asian elephants: the closest living relatives of woolly mammoths.

astrobiology: the study of life in the universe.

Atacama Desert: the desert located in the South American country of Chile, known as the driest place on Earth and home to extremophiles.

atmospheric pressure: the force created by the weight of the atmosphere.

barycenter: the point around which two objects orbit.

biosignature: anything that shows evidence of past or present life in an environment.

black hole: the final stage of life for stars 10 times more massive than the sun. Even light cannot escape their tremendous gravitational force.

Calisto: the second largest moon of Jupiter.

carbon monoxide: a greenhouse gas that is produced by burning of fossil fuels.

carnivore: an animal that eats other animals.

Cassini: the probe studying Saturn and its satellites, named after Italian astronomer and mathematician Giovanni Cassini.

causal loop: an effect of time travel in which the order in which things happen no longer makes sense.

causality: cause and effect, or the order in which things happen.

centrifuge: a spinning machine, used by astronauts to lessen effects of microgravity.

centripetal force: the force felt toward the center when moving in a circular path.

chatbot: a computer program designed to act like a human.

chemical rocket: a rocket that uses chemicals, such as hydrogen or kerosene, to produce thrust.

climate change: a change in weather patterns, which can happen through natural processes or be manmade.

cloning: the process of creating genetically identical organisms.

colony: in space travel, a permanent settlement in space or on a body other than Earth.

combustion chamber: a container where fuel and an oxidizer are ignited to produce thrust.

composognathus: a small, two-legged, meat-eating dinosaur that lived about 150 million years ago.

constant: something that doesn't change.

cosmic: of, from, or relating to the universe.

cosmic radiation: radiation that comes from sources other than the sun, such as black holes or supernova.

GLOSSARY

cosmic rays: high-energy radiation coming from outside the solar system.

cosmic speed limit: the speed of light. Nothing can move faster through space.

cryovolcanism: similar to volcanism, but instead of erupting molten rock, cryovolcanoes erupt water ice, ammonia, and methane.

cryptographer: someone who studies cryptography, the science of creating or cracking codes.

de-extinction: the process of bringing an extinct organism back to life.

decay: the process of rotting or decomposing of organisms such as plants and animals.

decompose: the process of rotting of living organisms.

desalinization: the process of removing salts from water to make it drinkable.

DNA: deoxyribonucleic acid, make up the blueprint for all living organisms.

Doppler spectroscopy: a method of looking for exoplanets that watches for small wobbles, or changes in a star's light produced by an orbiting planet.

double helix: the physical shape of DNA, which looks like a ladder twisted around itself.

Drake Equation: an equation created by professor Frank Drake that gives an estimate of the number of intelligent civilizations in the galaxy.

Earth analog: an exoplanet that is similar to Earth.

eclipse: the blocking of light by an object, such as a moon or a planet.

ecosystem: a group of living organisms that share an environment.

effector: anything that allows a robot to interact with the world.

electron: a subatomic particle with negative charge.

embryonic cell: a cell from an embryo that can develop into any type of cell.

Enceladus: a small moon of Saturn that may have an ocean under its icy surface.

ethics: the discussion between what is right and what is wrong, or morality.

Europa: a moon of Jupiter that may hold a giant under-ice ocean. Also the sixth-largest moon in the solar system.

EVA: stands for extravehicular activity, which is when an astronaut leaves the safety of their spacecraft or space station.

event horizon: a limit past which nothing can leave a black hole.

evolution: how organisms change and adapt over time.

exoplanet: a planet that orbits stars other than our sun.

expelled: to be forced out at a high speed.

extinct: when there are no living members of a species.

extremophile: an organism that can survive in environments that most others cannot.

first contact: the term for the first communication between humans and an alien civilization.

fissure: a deep separation in a geologic feature, such as a crack in the surface of a moon or planet.

fossil: the remains of prehistoric organisms where minerals replace organic material, making a copy of the remains in stone.

fragment: a small piece, such as a fragment of DNA.

frequency: the number of times the top, or crest, of a wave passes a certain point in an amount of time.

galactic: having to do with a galaxy.

GLOSSARY

Galileo: space probe launched in 1989 that studied the planet Jupiter and its satellites, named after Italian astronomer Galileo Galilei.

gamma radiation: very high-energy electromagnetic rays, which can be harmful to astronauts.

Ganymede: the largest moon of Jupiter and the largest moon in the solar system.

theory of general relativity: the warping of space and time due to gravity, a theory first proposed by Albert Einstein.

gene: a segment of DNA that contains instructions for specific proteins.

genetic disease: a disease caused by problems in an organism's genes.

genetic diversity: different or similar traits between two individuals in a species.

geneticist: a scientist who studies genetics, the science of heredity.

genome: all of the genes that are needed to create an organism.

gestation period: the time when an embryo begins to develop until birth.

Goldilocks Zone: the distance from a star at which liquid water could exist on a planet's surface.

GPS: stands for Global Positioning System, a network of satellites that can be used to find your location on Earth.

greenhouse: a building that protects plants from outside weather.

habitable: capable of supporting life.

habitable zone: the distance from a star at which liquid water could exist on a planet's surface.

habitat: the normal environment an organism lives in.

half-life: the length of time it takes for half of a substance to disappear.

HI-SEAS: stands for Hawaii Space Exploration Analog and Simulation, a simulation of long-term Mars missions in Hawaii.

hot Jupiter: a gas giant like Jupiter that orbits very close to its star.

humanoid: being human-like, having traits of a human.

hybrid: a mixture of genetic traits from two or more different organisms.

ice age: a period in time when the average surface temperature of Earth was much colder.

industrial: manufacturing, or building things, in factories.

inefficient: in rocketry, an engine that wastes energy instead of producing thrust.

inherent traits: traits that are passed on through genes.

ion engine: a type of propulsion that uses a very light gas and an electric field to produce thrust.

Kepler space telescope: a telescope launched in 2009 to search for exoplanets using the transit method.

laws of robotics: author Isaac Asimov created these laws in his *I, Robot* stories to control how robots treated humans.

light year: the distance light travels in one year.

liquid fuel: type of rocket engine in which liquid fuel and oxidizer are combined to produce thrust, which can be throttled.

luminosity: the total amount of energy emitted by a star.

magnetic field: on Earth, protects the surface by deflecting solar and cosmic radiation.

Mariner 4: the first probe to return up-close images of Mars in 1965.

Mars Science Laboratory (MSL): a roving science robot on Mars, also called *Curiosity*.

mass: a measurement of how much matter is in an object.

meteor: cosmic debris that enters Earth's atmosphere, also called a "shooting star."

meteorite: any part of a meteor that survives its flight through the atmosphere and lands on Earth.

methanogens: bacteria that don't need oxygen to survive and that produce methane.

microbe: a living organism that can be seen only with a microscope, such as bacteria.

microgravity: when the force of gravity is very weak.

moral: the discussion between what is right and what is wrong for a particular issue.

mutation: when a gene is damaged or changed to cause new traits.

neutron stars: the final stage of life for stars about twice as massive as the sun, which have gravity strong enough to combine protons and electrons into neutrons.

New Horizons: the first probe to study Pluto and its moons. Also the fastest rocket-propelled craft every made.

nuclear fusion: when atomic particles fuse together to make heavier particles and release energy, causing stars to shine.

nuclear thermal engine: highly efficient rocket engine designed for deep space, capable of traveling to Mars in weeks.

nuclear transfer: a method of cloning that removes DNA from an unfertilized egg and replaces it with the DNA of the organism to be cloned.

organic: material from a living organism.

ozone: a gas produced by engines and machines that can help cause smog.

paleontologist: a scientist that studies life in the distant past through fossils.

parthenogenesis: the ability to produce offspring without a mate.

payloads: part of a rocket that is intended to reach space to perform a task.

perchlorates: salts that lower the freezing point of water on Mars and that can be toxic to humans.

permafrost: a layer of soil in cold regions that stays frozen year-round.

photon: a particle of light.

Pleistocene Epoch: the time period from 2.6 million to 11,700 years ago when large mammals, such as the woolly mammoth, lived in cold, northern climates.

Polaris: the star closest to the north celestial pole, about 433 light years from Earth.

potable: water that is drinkable.

prehistoric: the time in history before written records were kept.

process: using a computer program that lets robots decide what to do based on information from its sensors.

Project Orion: proposed propulsion method that involves exploding nuclear bombs behind a spaceship.

propulsion: pushing or moving an object forward.

pulsars: long-dead, quickly spinning stars that emit pulses of electromagnetic energy.

quanta: in quantum physics, a specific amount of energy.

quantum mechanics: the physics of subatomic particles, which describes behavior that Newton's laws cannot.

radiation: a form of electromagnetic energy that can cause harm to living organisms.

GLOSSARY

radio astronomer: an astronomer who studies the universe using radio waves, which are a part of the electromagnetic spectrum.

recurring slope lineae (RSL): dark areas of Martian soil that were found to be made by liquid water.

reference point: in motion, a reference point lets you compare who is moving and who is not.

relative: compared to something else.

roboticist: a scientist that researches, studies, and creates robots.

Saturn V: the most powerful rocket ever flown, which was used to take men to the moon.

scale factor: a number that multiplies a measurement, which is useful in making models of very large or small things.

science fiction: a story about contact with other worlds and imaginary science and technology.

sediment: material-like sand or silt that is carried and deposited by water into layers.

sensor: anything that gives a robot information about its surroundings.

sentient: able to perceive and feel.

septillion: a 1 followed by 24 zeros.

SETI@Home: a citizen science project looking for radio signals from alien civilizations, which runs in the background on computers or as a screen saver.

Siberia: large northeastern area of Russia once home to woolly mammoths, steppe bison, and saber-toothed cats.

singularity: the center of a black hole, where matter is thought to be infinitely dense.

sol: the term for a Martian day, which is 37 minutes longer than a day on Earth.

solar eclipse: when the moon passes between the sun and the Earth.

solar flare: electromagnetic energy suddenly released by a star.

solid fuel: a type of rocket engine in which the oxidizer and fuel are already combined and that can't be throttled.

special relativity: the theory that describes how the laws of physics are always the same unless you are accelerating, and describes why the speed of light is the cosmic speed limit.

spectrometer: an instrument used to study the properties of light.

spectroscope: an instrument that measures the spectrum of light.

spectrum: the properties of a star's light that tell astronomers what it's made of and how to classify it.

subatomic particles: the group of particles that make atoms, such as neutrons, protons, and electrons.

sunspots: relatively cool areas on the surface of a star.

surrogate: an animal that gives birth to the young of another animal.

tactile: the sense of touch.

terraforming: the process of changing a planet to be more Earth-like.

terrestrial: an Earth-like planet with a rocky surface.

theoretician: in physics, someone who uses math to make models and predictions, rather than using actual experiments.

throttle: to control the amount of thrust.

thrust: the reaction force on a rocket that pushes it in the opposite direction from its exhaust.

tidal forces: the stretching and compressing of an object such as a moon by the gravity of a larger object, such as a planet.

timeline: the path of time in history.

traits: characteristics determined by DNA, such as being left-handed or right-handed.

transit: when a small object, such as a planet, blocks a small amount of light from a star.

tundra: a cold, mostly treeless area in very northern and very southern latitudes.

uncertainty principle: a theory first described by German physicist Werner Heisenberg, this property of quantum mechanics says that the more precisely the position of a particle is known, the less precisely its momentum can be known, and vice versa.

unstable: in wormholes, the inability to remain open long enough for anything to pass through.

Ursa Major: a familiar constellation of the northern hemisphere, part of which is called the Big Dipper.

variable: a value that can change.

viable: something that is usable

***Viking 1* and *Viking 2*:** twin spacecraft that landed on Mars in 1976 and returned the first pictures from the surface of Mars.

volcanic vents: openings in the Earth's crust where gases, lava, and rock can erupt.

volcanism: the eruption of molten rock, or magma, onto the surface of a planet through volcanoes and volcanic vents.

***Voyager*:** twin probes sent on a "grand tour" of the outer planets in 1977, carrying messages for intelligent civilizations.

warp drive: popular in science fiction, to bend space in such a way to make faster-than-light travel possible.

wavelength: the distance between the crests, or peaks, of a wave, which determines the type of electromagnetic radiation such as visible light and ultraviolet light.

weightlessness: the feeling of having no weight.

white dwarf: the final stage of life for a star the size of the sun.

woolly mammoth: a relative of modern elephants that lived in cold climates and went extinct about 3,000 years ago.

wormhole: a theoretical tunnel through space and time, predicted by relativity but never seen in real life.

Wrangel Island: an island of the northern coast of Siberia, home to the last group of woolly mammoths about 4,000 years ago.

xenon: a gas that is easily ionized and used in ion engines to create thrust.

METRIC CONVERSIONS

Use this chart to find the metric equivalents to the English measurements in this activity. If you need to know a half measurement, divide by two. If you need to know twice the measurement, multiply by two. How do you find a quarter measurement? How do you find three times the measurement?

ENGLISH	METRIC
1 inch	2.5 centimeters
1 foot	30.5 centimeters
1 yard	0.9 meter
1 mile	1.6 kilometers
1 pound	0.5 kilogram
1 teaspoon	5 milliliters
1 tablespoon	15 milliliters
1 cup	237 milliliters

RESOURCES

BOOKS

What's It Like in Space? Stories from Astronauts Who've Been There. Ariel Waldman, illustrated by Brian Standeford. Chronicle Books. San Francisco. 2016

Journey by Starlight: A Time Traveler's Guide to Life, the Universe, and Everything. Ian Flitcroft, illustrated by Britt Spencer. One Peace Books. Japan. 2013

WEBSITES

The Long Now Foundation is dedicated to preserving endangered species and bringing back those that have recently become extinct. Learn about the Long Now Foundation here.
reviverestore.org

Mars is the most studied object in the solar system, other than the Earth. Follow this link to see the past, present, and future of Mars exploration.
solarsystem.nasa.gov/missions/target/mars

Check out the Kepler space telescope page to learn more about Kepler's mission and the exoplanets found so far!
kepler.nasa.gov

Check out the SETI Institute's website, and keep up to date with the search for alien life!
seti.org

Have you ever wondered just how big space is? Check out this website to get a sense of the distances in our solar system!
joshworth.com/dev/pixelspace/pixelspace_solarsystem.html

Interested in cloning? Check out this link to learn how scientists cloned Dolly the sheep and other mammals.
pbslearningmedia.org/asset/biot09_int_cloning

Want to learn about coding, programming, and artificial intelligence? This website is full of fun resources.
kidscodecs.com

Science fiction or science fact? Check out this video to learn more about the facts behind the fiction!
youtube.com/watch?v=8yT3KetNU5A

What is science fiction? Watch this video to learn about the genre!
youtube.com/watch?v=nrusqQ5JftA

Ever wanted to help a scientist? Zooniverse is a website dedicated to citizen science—real science research you can do at home!
zooniverse.org

RESOURCES

QR CODE GLOSSARY

page 3: youtube.com/watch?v=Ii7uwp1SRIM

page 10: npr.org/sections/
thesalt/2016/01/11/462375558/our-
favorite-banana-may-be-doomed-
can-new-varieties-replace-it

page 11: retroreport.org/video/dolly-the-sheep

page 15: youtube.com/watch?v=D2IaIvf3rGo

page 17: whc.unesco.org/en/list/1023/gallery

page 20: youtube.com/watch?v=IWnlPYu3ovQ

page 24: genetics.thetech.org/online-
exhibits/do-it-yourself-strawberry-dna

page 24: youtube.com/watch?v=DaaRrR-ZHP4

page 27: robothalloffame.org/
inductees/03inductees/unimate.html

page 29: youtube.com/watch?v=J3edDaPSdY4

page 30: youtube.com/watch?v=qcqIYccgUdM

page 31: youtube.com/watch?v=rVlhMGQgDkY

page 32: youtube.com/watch?v=g0TaYhjpOfo

page 34: youtube.com/watch?v=g-dKXOlsf98

page 35: ted.com/talks/stephen_
hawking_asks_big_questions_about_
the_universe?language=en

page 37: youtube.com/watch?v=UnIFLIcBXOI

page 39: alice.pandorabots.com

page 39: cleverbot.com

page 40: lego.com/en-us/mindstorms/?do
mainredir=mindstorms.lego.com

page 40: vexrobotics.com

page 40: littlebits.cc

page 46: youtube.com/watch?v=P9VBkCpO-JU

page 49: instagram.com/stationcdrkelly/?hl=en

page 51: climatecentral.org/states-of-change#/nation

page 59: archive.org/details/OrsonWellesMrBruns

page 67: youtube.com/watch?v=YUj8upWN_Fg

page 68: exoplanets.nasa.gov

page 71: exoplanets.nasa.gov/news/1383/
eso-discovers-earth-size-planet-in-
habitable-zone-of-nearest-star

page 75: youtube.com/watch?v=q-yqVHrQP2Q

page 80: zooniverse.org

page 80: setiathome.ssl.berkeley.edu

page 85: youtube.com/watch?v=Pq7WmrTbi-Q

page 88: biography.com/people/
albert-einstein-9285408

page 91: ligo.caltech.edu/page/about

page 92: space.com/31901-historic-gravitational-
waves-discovery-explained-by-experts-video.html

page 101: youtube.com/watch?v=AM5EYO5wWMA

INDEX

INDEX